Governance of Colleges and Universities

THE CARNEGIE SERIES IN AMERICAN EDUCATION

The books in this series have resulted from studies made under grants from the Carnegie Corporation of New York and, occasionally, studies supported by The Carnegie Foundation for the Advancement of Teaching. These books are published by McGraw-Hill in recognition of their importance to the future of American education.

The Corporation, a philanthropic foundation established in 1911 by Andrew Carnegie for the advancement and diffusion of knowledge and understanding, has a continuing interest in the improvement of American education. It financed the studies in this series to provide facts and recommendations which would be useful to all those who make or influence the decisions which shape American educational policies and institutions.

The statements made and views expressed in these books are solely the responsibility of the authors.

Governance of Colleges and Universities

BY JOHN J. CORSON

McGRAW-HILL BOOK COMPANY, INC.

1960   New York   Toronto   London

GOVERNANCE OF COLLEGES AND UNIVERSITIES

78910111213 VB 1098

13201

ACKNOWLEDGMENTS

THE INQUIRY reported on in subsequent pages was undertaken at the suggestion of John W. Gardner, President, and James A. Perkins, Vice President, of the Carnegie Corporation. It was they who recognized the importance of the problems here explored, who supported the inquiry over what turned out to be a period of years rather than months, and who gave continual encouragement to the author.

In the observation of governance in the institutions used as samples, the author was aided by three individuals who gave generously of their time and opinions: John A. Perkins, President of the University of Delaware (whose experience contributed richly to the understanding of the functioning of other institutions); James D. Thompson, Director of the Administrative Science Center, University of Pittsburgh; and John H. Romani, then of the Brookings Institution, and now of the University of Pittsburgh.

In the preparation of this manuscript, the author was greatly aided by Dean Edwin D. Duryea, Jr., of Hofstra College. Dean Duryea contributed originally and substantially to the research that underlies this manuscript and to its writing and rewriting.

Finally I am indebted to four senior and respected students of higher education: Karl W. Bigelow, Professor of Education, Teachers College, Columbia University; W. H. Cowley, David Jacks Professor of Higher Education, Stanford University; Algo D. Henderson, Director, Center for the Study of Higher Educa-

tion, University of Michigan; and T. R. McConnell, Director of
the Center for the Study of Higher Education, University of California. Each of these scholars read the manuscript and contributed
materially by his insightful criticism and constructive suggestions.
Their aid has been substantial.

But the faults the reader will find here—in concept and in the
analysis of academic administration—are the author's. It is hoped
those faults may be outweighed by the value of a different look
at the functioning of colleges and universities. At the least, the
author has tried to look at these institutions with an appreciation
of their function and their environment and to subject them to
the kind of appraisal that as a professional management consultant
(as well as a several-time educator) he applies to clients in business and government. He hopes academic administrators, as well
as students of administration, will find this book useful.

John J. Corson

CONTENTS

Chapter 1

GOVERNING: ITS NATURE
AND SIGNIFICANCE

A MIRACLE IS NEEDED

AT NO TIME in this country's history have the institutions responsible for the higher education of this country's young men and women had a more important role to play than they have today. Indeed, as the President's Committee on Education Beyond the High School has pointed out, "Our colleges and universities are expected by the public to perform something close to a miracle in the next ten to fifteen years." [1]

The demand for this miracle comes not alone from the growth in population and the popularity of education. It comes, too, from the realization that only through adequate education can the United States remain the fabled land of democratic opportunity and achieve the level of civilization and economic strength that its resources and destiny promise. The magnitude and complexity of the challenge confronting the colleges and universities was succinctly suggested by the President's committee when it wrote: [2]

This nation has been propelled into a challenging new educational era since World War II by the convergence of powerful forces—an explosion

[1] *Second Report to the President,* The President's Committee on Education Beyond the High School, Washington, July, 1957, p. 3.

[2] *Ibid.,* p. 1.

1

of knowledge and economic advance, the outbreak of ideological conflict and the uprooting of old political and cultural patterns on a world-wide scale, and an unparalleled demand by Americans for more and better education.

It has been said that a country tends to support the kind of education necessary for its survival. If this principle applies throughout the period 1960 to 2000, it would necessitate:

1. The expansion of facilities for higher education to provide opportunities for the more than seven million students expected to enroll by 1970, an increase in enrollments of more than twofold. This burgeoning demand arises from the substantial increase in the birth rate during the 1940s and from the increasing proportion of all youth continuing education beyond the high school.

2. The adaptation to rapidly emerging social realities. Students must be equipped for the world of atoms, missiles, and new ideologies of 1960 to 2000.[3] This is a time, as others have written, when technologies become antiquated overnight.[4] To equip college students to live and to lead during the balance of the twentieth century will require a continuing reevaluation and enrichment of the courses and curricula through which they are trained to take their places in an evolving society. Each teacher, as he has always been obligated to do, must continually seek out new truth while he transmits what is known to his students. Yet, as John A. Perkins has pointed out, "Most of this creative work [in the humanistic fields], with notable exceptions, is done outside the university."[5]

[3] "The history of higher education shows that its institutions have alienated themselves from the spirit of their period or have decayed into glorified trade schools whenever they have not seen the necessity of a productive interaction between scholarship and human culture." Robert Ulich, "The American University and Changing Philosophies of Education," a chapter in Charles Frankel (ed.), *Issues in University Education*, Harper & Brothers, New York, 1959, p. 46.

[4] *The Pursuit of Excellence*, Panel Report V of the Special Studies Project, Rockefeller Brothers Fund, Inc., Doubleday & Company, Inc., New York, 1958, p. 11.

[5] John A. Perkins, "The Second Academic Mile," an address at the dinner honoring faculty authors at Temple University, Apr. 26, 1958.

3. The continued broadening of the functions of many institutions to serve a variety of cultural, vocational, and other needs of the community.[6] These institutions have been broadened in the past as the needs of society for trained teachers, for nurses, for pharmacists, or for business administrators have caused the establishment of a variety of specialized institutions. The need for such adaptation will be as great in the future.

In the decades ahead each college and university will be expected, as in the past, to advance and disseminate knowledge. In addition, these institutions will be confronted during the years ahead with demands for assistance from many groups within the community. Adults will look to these institutions for opportunities for continuing their education. Business will look to these institutions for the specialized training of employees, for technical advice in many fields, and for creative research on its problems. Government will look to these institutions for an increasing amount of research in many fields, for the training of young men destined to serve in the military forces, for the provision of technical advice to public projects at home and abroad, and for the support and development of institutions of higher learning in the underdeveloped countries.

The next four decades will place unprecedented demands on this country's 1,900 colleges and universities for (1) adaptability, (2) expansibility, and (3) creativity. To meet those demands administrators and faculty, both, must find improved ways of enlisting all members of the enterprise—trustees, academic and administrative officers, faculty members, librarians, and maintenance employees—in a dynamically improving collaborative effort. That effort must be equal to eliminating inflexible and tradition-bound practices, whether they have to do with the size of the institution or of its classes—with their traditional disciplines of knowledge—or with established notions about the institution's clientele. And that effort

[6] "Our basic problems in education derive from the total intellectual climate of our culture; to be effective education must relate itself constructively to the basic value questions of our age." Huston Smith, *The Purposes of Higher Education*, Harper & Brothers, New York, 1955, p. 6.

presumes that a working consensus will be reached among all members of the institution—trustees, officers, faculty—about what purpose is to be achieved by their institution.[7]

The college or university as a form of social organization—as an enterprise dedicated to the achievement of various purposes—has been subjected to little orderly analysis. Analysis of the functioning of business enterprises and governmental units has become commonplace and generally inclusive in character. The college or university as a functioning organism has less frequently been subjected to analysis, and then not often in terms of its total operations. The purpose of this study is to identify those analyses which promise to be most fruitful in revealing how the college or university as a social organism can be made more adequate to the demands of the decades ahead.

ORGANIZATION FOR EXPANDING DEMANDS

The organizational forms and practices through which each of these 1,900 colleges and universities seeks to make effective the effort of the congeries of individuals that constitute its total staff are unique in significant respects.[8] This uniqueness has its roots in academic tradition. But this uniqueness arises too from the nature

[7] Paul H. Davis, in an article entitled "All the World Stands Aside," declares that in visiting forty "exceptional" colleges and universities over a ten-year period he found "two items which appeared to be paramount . . . (1) clearly defined objectives and (2) missionary zeal." And he placed especial stress on the value of "clearly defined objectives." *Association of American Colleges Bulletin*, 43(2): 269–273, 1957.

[8] An excellent historical analysis of the origins of the organizational forms of this country's colleges and universities is included in a series of lectures on "American Academic" given by Prof. W. H. Cowley of Stanford University at the University of Illinois in the spring of 1959. Here is the fullest and most authoritative statement to be found in the literature of academic government on the nature of the government of the early Italian, French, Dutch, and English universities. And here is an excellent analysis of the origin in early American universities of the institutions of the "governing board," the "board of visitors," the "presidency," and the "chancellor," and of the authority of the faculty.

of the functions performed by an educational enterprise; they are different functions requiring a different organization and different practices than are common in business or governmental enterprises.

The substantial growth in the size and complexity of many educational institutions leads one to ask whether these organizational forms and practices are adequate to enable these institutions to meet tomorrow's problems. Indeed, there is increasing evidence that growth in enrollments and "the multiplying educational needs and demands of American society" make essential a new evaluation of the adequacy of the curriculum, teaching methods, administrative process, financial management, and organizational structure.[9]

The organizational forms and practices of the earlier colleges in this country are summarized by John Dale Russell in the following words: [10]

Until the last quarter of the Nineteenth Century the pattern of internal administrative organization in the institutions of higher education in the United States was simple. The enrollment of almost every institution was small by today's standards. The curriculum was standardized and consisted almost exclusively of required subjects with limited substitutions allowed in the "classical" course for students taking the "modern" or "scientific" course. The "faculty" consisted of a president and rarely more than three or four other professors. Such a situation did not require an administrative organization and the president was the only official with executive responsibilities.

As the substance of education has steadily expanded and the size of institutions has grown manyfold, there has necessarily evolved an ever more complex structure of university organization. Today the modern university offers the student the opportunity to sample learning in many subdivisions of these original fields through perhaps a dozen schools and a multiplicity of subject-matter departments. In contrast to the small body of students that in the past attended even the largest institution, the numbers have now greatly

[9] See editorial comment in *AAUP Bulletin*, spring, 1957.
[10] "Changing Patterns of Administration," *The Annals*, September, 1956.

expanded. Within the recent past, i.e., from 1930 to 1958, the number of institutions having—

    0 to   499 students has increased by one-tenth
  500 to 2,999 students has approximately doubled
3,000 to 9,999 students has increased nearly threefold
10,000 or more students (while small in total) has similarly
    increased nearly threefold

A college or university today with an enrollment of 1,000 or more students (and approximately 33 per cent of all accredited institutions have enrollments this large) includes a faculty of from 75 to 4,000 or more. Even a faculty of 75 no longer can resolve many of its problems by face-to-face dealing. It has established academic officers (registrars, deans of students, and others) to handle problems once handled by the president or controlled by the faculty as a body, and it is aided by administrative officers (comptrollers, purchasing agents, and superintendents of buildings and grounds) who decide other questions that once were largely the responsibility of the body of scholars that constituted the whole staff of the institution.

Throughout the period of growth there has been a conscious effort in most institutions to preserve the values which obtained under the traditional faculty-centered form of organization. Yet there are substantial evidences that this effort has been unsuccessful. On the one hand, college and university presidents complain about the limitations placed upon their exercise of executive discretion by the power of the faculty. On the other hand, some faculty members complain that their status is no longer as substantial, nor as dignified.

The cause may be found in their own abdication of areas of responsibility, e.g., student counseling, but the complaint of the faculty members is none the less lusty. Frederick D. Wilhelmsen, for example, writes of the "alienated professor" who, having once had complete jurisdiction over admissions and studies, now "finds himself in a hideously ambivalent situation wherein his ancient rights have withered under the clinical efficiency of a university which has ceased to be a republic of learning and which has largely become an employer of technicians and specialists." [11]

GOVERNING—ITS NATURE

The professors' plaint is a manifestation of the universal impulse to freedom. The individual, at least in a democratic society, continually aspires for the right to choose between alternatives. He derives a sense of power if he can but impose his own will on the direction of events. He gains a feeling of personal dignity and worthwhileness if he can influence those events which concern his being and his future. The professor who enjoyed a greater right to choose the students he would teach, to decide what he would teach them, and to determine many other questions about the work he did in an educational institution controlled in considerable part by the faculty, now resents what he regards as a loss of freedom he once possessed.

In a society that includes many people—be it a nation or a city, a business or a university—freedom exists for the individual only when order prevails. Order among human beings may be the result of habit or may be established by rules of governments. The habit of reporting for work, lunching, and concluding the day's work at certain times makes for order among the group. Rules that all shall behave in a stipulated manner and shall work toward stated ends similarly establish order.

In each society—the nation, the city, the business, or the university—someone must make rules to govern the conduct of and the relations among those who are banded together—in living together within a nation or city, or in accomplishing certain ends, as in the business or the university. In this sense, not only the nation and the city are "governments" but so are the business and the university. Each makes "rules" that "govern" the individuals that make up the group, telling them what shall be done, how, and when. Within the law, the business or the university is authorized

[11] Frederick D. Wilhelmsen, "The Alienated Professor," *Commonweal*, Apr. 6, 1956, pp. 10–11.

and organized to make rules for the conduct of its affairs. Thus each maintains order and certainty among the group and facilitates the achievement of whatever it is established to do. But like other governments, neither can afford order or certainty if it is achieved at the cost of the freedom of those who are governed. Business and the university, like, or perhaps to a greater degree than, the nation or the state, must obtain the consent of the governed.

The idea that any institution which makes rules to govern the conduct of individuals is itself a government is not a new one. It was advanced first by Charles Meriam, the distinguished professor of political science at the University of Chicago in the 1930s.[12] It was applied to the business enterprise in imaginative terms by Beardsley Ruml, erstwhile scholar, professor, businessman, and scholar again, in 1945.[13] The idea was developed in relation to the functioning of the labor union by Prof. Philip Taft of Brown University in 1954.[14] It has been applied to the functioning of military organizations by a number of scholars. And it has been used to interpret the structure and functioning of the Catholic Church.[15]

GOVERNING OF A UNIVERSITY

The idea that an institution is a government, in the sense that it is authorized to make rules that govern the conduct of individuals, is especially useful in the analysis of the functioning of a college or university. The college or university is like other institutions—like a business, a labor union, or a family—in important respects. It is unlike such institutions in other significant respects.

The college or university has in common with other groups of human beings four common characteristics:

[12] Charles E. Meriam, *Public and Private Government,* Yale University Press, New Haven, Conn., 1944.

[13] Beardsley Ruml, *Tomorrow's Business,* Rinehart & Company, Inc., New York, 1945.

[14] Philip Taft, *The Structure and Government of Labor Unions,* Harvard University Press, Cambridge, Mass., 1954.

[15] E. M. Lynskey, *The Government of the Catholic Church,* P. J. Kenedy & Sons, New York, 1952.

1. It exists to accomplish something; it has a purpose or purposes. The purpose or purposes for which the enterprise came into being may have been changed, expanded, or lost sight of, but it exists for a purpose.

2. It must have resources. These may, in oversimplified terms, be described as men, money, and materials. Whatever they are— skilled scientists, teachers, working capital, endowment, oil reserves, or books in the library—there are resources essential to the accomplishment of each group of human beings that work together.

3. It must have processes that facilitate men and women working together to accomplish a purpose. The process may have to do with the admission of students to a college, the drawing of stocks from inventory in a manufacturing plant, or the determination that an aged person is entitled to a governmental pension. The point is that if human beings are to work together effectively (and especially in a large organization), a process must exist which enables each to do his part in concert with others. Think of that point in relation to the functioning of a football team, and then in relation to the taking of an order in Teheran for a machine to sort punched cards to be made in Endicott, New York, by the International Business Machines Corporation.

4. The enterprise moves on—it grows or it retrogresses. Change is a common characteristic of large enterprises. All facets of the human enterprise—its purposes, its resources and their utilization, its processes, and the responsibility for making decisons about each —continually undergo change.

The college or university differs from other forms of enterprise in three significant respects:

1. Colleges and, to a still greater degree, universities exist to serve a multiplicity of purposes. Viewed from the standpoint of the institution, a college exists to educate students, to carry on research, to mold the characters and values of the students it educates, and perhaps periodically to put on athletic spectacles. Viewed through the eyes of the parents, it exists to educate students, but as well to improve their social standing and, perhaps, to find them jobs. Viewed from the standpoint of the neighboring industry, it

may exist to do research on "practical problems" and to provide training facilities for the industry's employees. Viewed through the eyes of the alumni, it exists to provide educational opportunities for their children and to present annually a football team and various athletic events.

2. The college, and to a lesser degree the university, is more dispersed as an enterprise than the typical business enterprise or governmental agency. Any group of human beings existing to accomplish a purpose, and particularly the larger groups, includes subdivisions that exist to perform separate although related functions. The university includes many and relatively independent schools, colleges, institutes, and departments. Governance is, in considerable part, the task of establishing rules and making the succession of decisions that are required to relate these subdivisions, of assuring order, and hopefully productive association, among them.

3. The responsibility for making decisions is more widely diffused. The operation of a college or university involves the continual making of decisions on what courses shall be taught (and not taught); how many books can be bought; what research shall be undertaken; what teams shall be coached (and to what end); how much money shall be allocated to teachers, coaches, maintenance staffs, and others; by whom classes shall be taught, libraries operated, and dining rooms run; and how and from whom additional income will be raised. The very listing of such decisions, and many others that must be made almost daily, suggests the wide range of deans, department heads, teachers, coaches, and others in whom effective responsibility for decision making rests.

THE NATURE OF DECISION MAKING

The diffusion of responsibility for the decision making that constitutes the governing of a college or university must be considered in the light of a clear understanding of what *decision making* is.

John Locke and Montesquieu, as well as current-day students of administration, have emphasized the importance, in studying the functioning of an enterprise, of distinguishing between the processes of *deciding* how an enterprise shall be run and of *doing* what has been decided shall be done.[16] In any enterprise—business, governmental, or educational—the responsibility of *doing* is widely distributed among those who make up the enterprise. In business and governmental enterprises the responsibility for *deciding* is less widely distributed. It is centered in a chief executive who may choose to delegate limited authority for making some decisions to a limited number of individuals. To the extent it is delegated, ways must be found, in day-to-day operation, to integrate the energies, initiative, and zeal of all who share the responsibility for making decisions. That integration is recognition of the fact that the "making" of an organizational decision is not often an instantaneous act by an individual. It is usually a process in which the ideas, analyses, and factual contributions of many individuals may be assembled for final approval or decision by an executive.[17]

The process of deciding is distinctive in the college or university in the degree to which *final* responsibility for making decisions is diffused. Substantial independent authority for making various types of decisions is allocated beyond the trustees and the president to the faculty as a group, to individual teachers, to department heads, to deans, to coaches, and to administrative officers. It follows, hence, that the government of a college or university poses distinctive problems in finding ways of enlisting and integrating the energies, initiative, and zeal of the relatively larger number among whom responsibility for decision making is shared.

THE PROBLEM TO BE EXAMINED

The wide variety of decisions made in the operation of a university or college can be classified in six broad categories: educational

---

[16] See, for example, H. A. Simon, *Administrative Behavior*, The Macmillan Company, New York, 1947.

[17] "An executive decision is only a moment in a process. The growth of decision, the accumulation of authority, not the final step, is what we need most to study." Mary Parker Follett, "The Meaning of Responsibility in Business Management," a paper included in Henry C. Metcalf and L. Urwick, *Dynamic Administration*, Harper & Brothers, New York, 1940, p. 146.

and research program; student affairs; faculty affairs; external relations, i.e., alumni, legislative, and general public relations; finance (current and capital); and physical development.[18] The subgroups or parts of the college or university which tend to make many decisions and conduct their affairs in an autonomous fashion are the colleges, departments, schools, and sometimes divisions.

This exploratory study is concerned with the manner in which the responsibility for making decisions in each of these six categories is distributed, and how the efforts of all—trustees, administrators, faculty, and staff—are mobilized in the progressive operation of the whole institution. More simply stated, this study is concerned with such questions as: By whom and how are decisions in each category made at a variety of institutions? How, for example, are decisions made, and how should they be made, in questions concerning the appointment of individuals to tenure posts; the selection of department heads, deans, and presidents; the raising of tuition; and the establishment of a new school?

What significant problems arise out of the manner in which authority to make decisions is entrusted to, or denied to, the faculty, the department heads, the deans, the administrators (treasurer, business manager, comptroller), the president, and the trustees? And particularly, what improvements are required in the organization and management processes of the typical university if, to use the words of Chester I. Barnard, "conscious, deliberate, purposeful cooperation" among trustees, academic officers, administrative officers, and faculty is to make possible more dynamic, enterprising educational effort?

The exploratory study reported upon here has been concerned, in short, with that administrative process which in the university or college is distinctive, the process of *deciding* and of seeing to it that the decisions made are executed. To this process we apply the term *governance;* [19] that is, we are examining the process or art

---

[18] This categorization is borrowed, in principal part, from ideas voiced in conversations by John D. Millett; its testing in the institutions studied confirms its practicality for this usage.

[19] The term *governance* is defined (*Oxford English Dictionary,* 1939, and

with which scholars, students, teachers, administrators, and trustees associated together in a college or university establish and carry out the rules and regulations that minimize conflict, facilitate their collaboration, and preserve essential individual freedom.

BASES FOR STUDYING GOVERNANCE

This study of the governance of American colleges and universities has been based, in part, on the limited observation of the governing processes in a number of institutions. Some institutions whose functioning was observed at first hand are described in Appendix A (with vital statistics indicating their general characteristics). No effort was made to visit and study a "representative sample" of *all* institutions of higher education, including state colleges, junior colleges, technological institutes, and others. Whatever claim can be made for the general applicability of the analyses of governance that are offered in subsequent chapters rests on two additional bases.

In addition to the observation of the governance of those institutions listed in Appendix A, this volume presents the results of conversations and correspondence with a number of authorities in the administration of higher education and with many college and university trustees, presidents, deans, and teachers who gave of their time and ideas generously. In addition, it is founded on the study of much of the large and expanding body of literature that touches or deals with the administration of colleges and universities.

This mounting body of literature depicts the functioning, today and in the past, of institutions of higher learning and offers meaningful insights into their governance. In the aggregate, this body of literature is voluminous. Yet, to glean from this mass how the power to make decisions with respect to educational and research program, student affairs, faculty affairs, external relations, i.e., governmental and public relations, finance (current and capital), and physical development is distributed and exercised requires the care-

---

White's Political Dictionary, 1949) as "the process or art of governing" and "the action or manner of governing."

ful marshaling of bits and pieces from many works. No student of the administration of higher education has effectively revealed how and why the power is distributed among trustees, president, deans, department heads, and faculty as it typically is in this country's institutions of higher learning. Nor has there been an effective assessment of the strengths and weaknesses that accrue from the distribution of authority that is customary.

LOOKING FORWARD

The inadequacy of both bases for the study of governing that have been pictured—observation of the functioning of a limited number of institutions of several types, and the gleaning of bits and pieces from a vast variety of writings about colleges and universities—lies in the fact that neither offers a foundation for a look forward. And to look forward to the kind of governance that will be required in the decade ahead, when the numbers to be educated in these institutions will have doubled, is essential. Hence, the author has tried, in the chapters that follow, to visualize not only what is the nature of the processes of governance that have obtained, but what are the characteristics of the academic enterprise that dictate the kinds of governance that shall prevail in the future.

Before the problems of governance can be better understood, those characteristics which distinguish the college or university as a social organization must be identified. Hence, Chapter 2 pictures those characteristics which must be accommodated in whatever system of governance obtains. Colleges and universities have been hurt more often than helped by well-meaning trustees and alumni who would "straighten the place out" by applying tried and true business methods to activities that such methods do not fit, and who would deal with faculties without realizing that teachers tend to think and act and be motivated differently than the typical business work force.

Similarly, to understand the governance of colleges and universities requires recognition of the fact that the *scalar principle*,[20] so firmly imbedded in the minds of those acquainted with business, governmental, and military organizations, has no duplicate in the academic enterprise. The roles of the trustees, the president, the deans, the department heads, and the faculty (or faculties) have a surface similarity to the scalar organization found in other enterprises, but a basic dissimilarity. It is, in considerable part, with these basic and subtle dissimilarities that Chapters 3 to 5 deal when they review, in turn, the roles of university-wide officers, academic officers, and the faculties.

As pointed out earlier, the college or university, like other forms of enterprise, must "have processes that facilitate men and women working together to accomplish a purpose." But are the processes by which a president gets things done through a faculty and the attendant staff of a college or university different from those by which the chief executive of a corporation or the chief of a governmental bureau stimulates the productivity of his staffs? And, especially, if the processes do differ, why? Chapter 6 endeavors to answer these questions. Perhaps even more usefully, it points out the especially fruitful opportunities that exist for scholars of academic administration who will analyze and devise—not describe—the peculiar nature of the processes that are required in the governance of colleges and universities.

Chapter 7 explores the nature and weight of the influences that are exercised by external groups—alumni, government, accrediting associations, foundations, donors, and others—on those within the institution who are responsible for making decisions. Consideration is given to the manner in which the institution adapts its curriculum, its courses, and its processes to the significant developments in the society it serves as reflected by these external groups, and simultaneously to how the institution maintains its integrity by resisting

[20] The scalar principle has been defined as "the grading of duties, not according to different functions but according to degrees of authority and corresponding responsibility." James D. Mooney, *The Principles of Organization,* Harper & Brothers, New York, rev. ed., 1947, p. 14.

proposals that would distort its basic educational program and objectives.

In the last analysis a college or university is a whole, not a collection of unrelated parts, as autonomous as some schools or departments may seem at times. Hence, in the concluding chapter attention is turned to the elements which give wholeness to the governance of a college or university. The nature of "institutional character" is pictured and explored. And here the nature of the peculiar
brand of leadership that is effective in academic governance is considered.

A FURTHER COMMENT

George Williams, in his delightfully provocative book, *Some of
My Best Friends Are Professors*,[21] argues that:

In the days when the colleges affected only a fraction of the population,
it did not matter much what they did—whether they stagnated or pro-
gressed, whether they taught well or ill. But the time is upon us when it
does matter. Very soon the vast majority of Americans will go to college;
those who do not go will have children who go; and every man and woman
will be paying stiff taxes to help support the colleges. It is essential, therefore, that the American college be examined carefully with a view to our
discovering whether it is worthy of the destiny it has just before it, as well
as of the trust we must put in it as the chief defender of our nation and
of our civilization in the days to come.

Harold W. Stoke made the same basic point when he wrote that
"higher education in the United States is now compulsory. It
became compulsory when we began to realize that the nation could
not survive without it." [22] If this be the case—and certainly it is—
the importance of its well-being is obvious.

The well-being of higher education, its progressive development

[21] *Some of My Best Friends Are Professors: A Critical Commentary on Higher
Education*. Abelard-Schuman, Ltd., New York, 1958.
[22] *The American College President*, Harper & Brothers, New York, 1959,
p. vii.

to keep pace with the evolution of our society, depends heavily on the effectiveness of the governance of each college and university. That requisite to educational progress has been the subject of little orderly analysis in the past. In succeeding chapters, I will identify the distinctive nature of the problems of college and university governance that cry out for analysis—and hopefully will persuade others to go to work on these problems.

Chapter 2

THE UNIVERSITY AS AN
ADMINISTRATIVE ENTERPRISE

ORGANIZATIONAL DILEMMA: ORDER VS. ENTERPRISE

As INSTITUTIONS grow large and complex—be the institution an industrial firm, a business enterprise, a religious institution, a government bureau, or a university—each faces a plaguing dilemma. Can it, on the one hand, develop a systematic organization to coordinate all its members in achieving its purpose while, on the other hand, stimulating and facilitating the enterprise of each member?

To answer this question with respect to the college or university requires an understanding of the distinctive characteristics of the context within which it operates. That context is formed by the function or purposes, the participants, the resources, the structure, i.e., the *parts* (schools, colleges, and departments), and the external groups that create, influence, or support the institution. And administrative practice and procedure must be designed in full recognition of this context. As one sage observer has commented, "Administrative absurdity increases directly with the square of the distance between context and process." [1]

[1] Earl Latham, professor of political science, Amherst College, in a letter to the author, Apr. 19, 1959.

CHARACTERISTICS OF PURPOSE

If a group of human beings are to work together effectively within an enterprise, students of administration contend, each must understand and share a common concern in achieving the purpose or purposes for which the enterprise exists. Does the context within which the American college or university exists facilitate or impede the establishment of such understanding and concern?

Multiplicity of Purposes

The American college or university exists to serve not a single purpose, but several. It exists to instruct students, and it may strive simultaneously to offer training in the liberal arts, advanced training in the scholarly disciplines, training in the professions, continuing education for adults, and still other forms of instruction. It exists, too, to carry on research, both pure and applied. It exists to provide a variety of student services, ranging from feeding, housing, and medical care to the provision of recreational opportunities, vocational counseling, and assistance in finding employment. And it is called upon to provide a wide range of community services.

Faculty members and administrative officers who comprise the staff of an American college or university have a common orientation in their concern with knowledge in a broad sense. Each in his way is engaged in an effort to develop, communicate, and conserve knowledge of mankind's cultural heritage, physical environment, and future potentialities.

But each faculty member and most administrative officers are engaged in separable, specialized activities that make up the work of a modern college or university. In the small liberal arts college, faculty members are distributed among twenty or more disciplines —anthropology to zoology—and within these disciplines faculty members have more or less specialized interests. Their colleagues in the administration, meanwhile, have quite different responsibilities. In the university, in addition to individuals widely specialized in the disciplines, faculty members are often grouped in separate and competing philosophical groups. The humanists differ with the scientists on central educational questions, and both differ with the social scientists. All of these differ with the members of the professional faculties. Indeed, their intellectual differences are intensified by the relative status or prestige that one philosophical clique accords to another.

The task of gaining consensus on what an institution shall be and how it should carry on its work is made difficult by this broad range of activities, by the various interests of many specialists, by the relative independence of many of the activities that are carried on, and by the inherent nature of many teachers (e.g., a professor, it has been said, is a man who thinks otherwise). The problems raised for decision by this diversity of activities are further complicated by a wide variety of opinion on what a university should be and do. This difference of opinion makes itself apparent in the decision-making councils on many issues.

Teachers of the liberal arts differ with other teachers who are more vocationally oriented about what should be included in the four-year curriculum properly to prepare students for their careers. Faculty members are hired to teach, but gain esteem and advancement by their research achievement. The academic activities associated with teaching and research compete for funds with auxiliary activities such as athletics, residences, and student services. Stress is placed upon the university's responsibility to encourage superior students in order to provide society with its future leaders, yet a greater proportion of time and energy is claimed by the necessity of assisting the less competent.

At the same time, members of society at large look to colleges and universities for a wide variety of direct services along with instruction.[2] Powerful constituencies—business, agriculture, and individual professions—expect these institutions, and particularly the state university, to provide both specialized training and research for their members; consider, for example, the activities of the schools of Agriculture, Industrial and Labor Relations, and Nutrition at

[2] See, for example, "The *Fortune* Survey on Higher Education," a special insert reporting the results of surveys by Elmo Roper, *Fortune*, September, 1949.

Cornell University or the activities of a number of the land-grant colleges. Informed people recognize the importance of maintaining campuses as centers for scholars holding widely differing philosophical and intellectual commitments. Within the educational program, students expect to take subjects which range the length of the alphabet. Within each discipline, differing points of view characterize and are expected to characterize members of the department.

Decision making takes place, therefore, in an atmosphere of differences of opinion as well as diversity of function. Academic and administrative officers are continually confronted with the task of combining this diversity in a succession of decisions that give a consistent unity and sense of purpose to the functioning of the institution. That they often fail to accomplish this is suggested by Litchfield in the following words: [3]

> There are few among us who regard the university as a total institution. It would be more accurate to say that we treat it as a miscellaneous collection of faculties, research institutes, museums, hospitals, laboratories, and clinics. Indeed, it has become a commonplace to observe that most of our large university organizations are held together by little more than a name, a lay board of trustees, an academically remote figure called a president, and a common concern for the power plant. On most of our large university campuses, our individual faculties tend to live in isolated proximity.

Among the consequences of such fragmentation of the university he lists: the development of some faculties at the expense of others, the neglect of liberal education in order to meet the needs of the professional and technical schools, marked discrepancies in standards among faculties on the same campus, the donation of funds to marginal activities because the needs of the whole institution are not effectively presented, the submerging of one or more basic disciplines in a single professional school, and the lack of interdisciplinary teaching and research programs.

The ideal structure and process that Litchfield and others picture for the university is described in the *Report of the President's Com-*

[3] Edward H. Litchfield, "The University: A Congeries or an Organic Whole?" *AAUP Bulletin*, September, 1959, pp. 375–376.

mittee on the Educational Future of the [*Columbia*] *University* as follows: [4]

> . . . It must be so organized that no level of instruction is neglected. It must be so arranged that each specialized part can draw easily upon the resources of the other parts. . . . To these tasks any particular university should be capable of bringing a sense of mission that enables it to select what it will emphasize as a deliberate policy. Such a selective emphasis has to be applied at the center and felt in all the parts from which come most of the impulses of growth. All of this involves the structure, procedures and pervasive awareness that bind the parts to the whole and to each other. In addition, as much as in any other form of human association and in a peculiarly sensitive way, the union amid diversity sought in a university must relate the individual member to the organization. Without unduly diverting the scholar from teaching and research, the university must draw his judgment into the work of the administrators.

These words picture a theoretically desirable goal. Is it achievable? When one views the functioning of American universities and, to a lesser degree, some colleges, the fundamental question arises whether they can serve as many purposes as most of them accept responsibility for and still achieve organic unity. Or is such unity only possible within component divisions?

Evaluating the Product

A second characteristic of the purpose which places distinctive demands upon the administrative practice and procedure of the college and university is the relative (in contrast with business or government) difficulty of evaluating the quality of the product. The crucial activity for which these institutions exist takes place in the minds and characters of individuals—faculty members and students. It cannot readily be measured as a basis for exercising administrative control or for evaluating individual performance. The overwhelming assumption of positions of power and importance in American society by college graduates attests unquestionably to the significance of higher education. The role of the scientist in

[4] Arthur W. Macmahon, executive director, *The Report of the President's Committee on the Educational Future of the University*, The Trustees of Columbia University, in the city of New York, 1957, p. 21.

modern society likewise evidences the achievement of scholarship and research, as do the contributions of academicians in a wide variety of fields which range from art through the social sciences. The succession of significant research findings that flow from university offices and laboratories is a further evidence of the importance of these institutions and their staffs.

The problem for decision making lies in the difficulty of evaluating the contribution to product of the various factors of production, of which the faculty is one, and of evaluating the particular individual in terms of the effectiveness of his contribution.

Evaluation of teaching and of decisions on questions which relate to the effect of the educational process on the students' minds presents special complexities. For scholarship and research the problem seems simpler than for teaching. Publication in professional journals, textbooks, and other mechanisms for communication provide concrete evidences for evaluation, at least by colleagues in a discipline if not by administrators and others. Yet it is still difficult to measure the quality of this product as well as its quantity.

There have been frequent attempts to appraise the university's product in terms of graduates' earnings; [5] others attempt to gauge institutional accomplishment in terms of the placement of graduates. [6] Some studies have directed attention to the number of alumni of particular institutions that have been stimulated to continue their training beyond the college. [7] *American Men of Science, Directory of American Scholars, Who's Who,* and similar references are used as measures of the accomplishment of institutions in terms

[5] U.S. Chamber of Commerce, *Education: An Investment in People,* Washington, 1956.

[6] Figures 6 and 7 in *Teacher Supply and Demand in Colleges and Universities,* a study conducted by the Research Division, National Education Association, Washington, 1957.

[7] Robert H. Knapp and H. B. Goodrich, *Origins of American Scientists,* a study made under the direction of a committee of the faculty of Wesleyan University, the University of Chicago Press, for Wesleyan University, copyright 1952 by the University of Chicago. Also Robert H. Knapp and Joseph J. Greenbaum, *The Younger American Scholar, His Collegiate Origins,* the University of Chicago Press and the Wesleyan University Press, Inc., for Wesleyan University, copyright 1953 by the University of Chicago.

of the success of their graduates. In recent years a few studies have attempted to measure what influence is exerted by institutions of higher education upon the values held by students.[8] Such studies provide useful information on faculty effectiveness and the worth of the educational program in various times in the past, but afford no precise and generally accepted measure of the effectiveness with which the function of a particular university is now being performed.

The effectiveness of universities and colleges, to a greater degree than that of their institutional counterparts in business and government, can be evaluated only many years after the fact. The production of enlightened graduates and the fruitfulness of the research performed by faculty members can be evaluated only after considerable time has elapsed. By then these institutions frequently have undergone substantial change, as have conditions in society. And then the results of evaluation are of little aid to faculties and administrative officers in deciding how individual colleges, schools, and departments should revise curricula, teaching, or other processes now.

The evaluation of the college or university's product, of the performance of its faculty, is made especially difficult by the very nature of the relationship of the professor to his students. The effectiveness of the professor is not measured by his effects on the institution, but by the change in the student. The initiative for the action by which this change takes place rests with the student. While the professor is expected to stimulate such initiative and guide the change in the student, his success depends, in considerable part, on the quality of the students he works with. The relationship remains, as described by St. Thomas Aquinas, like that of the doctor who cannot cure the patient's body, but can only help it to cure itself.

[8] See, for example, Philip E. Jacob, *Changing Values in College,* The Edward W. Hazen Foundation, New Haven, Conn., 1957. See also Nevitt Sanford (ed.), "Personality Development during the College Years," *Journal of Social Issues,* 12(4):1–70, 1956. This study lists five other studies from which "the most revealing data as to American student values come."

The administration of a university involves a wide range of problems for which little tangible evidence is yet available to assist the administrator in making decisions. The dean or department head has few objective measures of the teacher's effectiveness; the student may not recognize his teacher's worth until years after graduation; and the general public is not in a position to evaluate knowingly.

Within the institution itself, policies having to do with large versus small classes, residential versus commuting programs, lecture method versus discussion in teaching, democratic versus authoritarian attitudes toward students, and many similar matters are founded in large part on value judgments unaided by definite criteria. Values associated with such phrases as "scholarly research," "academic standards," "academic freedom," "liberal arts requirements," and "content courses" dominate discussion rather than factual analysis of the consequences of possible courses of action.

With few tangible guides to aid the judgment of the president, dean, or department head, decision making in matters of educational program, teachers and teaching, student development, the worth of research, or even budgetary and building requirements is made the more difficult.

CHARACTERISTICS OF THE PARTICIPANTS

Because of the size of the modern university, a faculty with 1,000 to 5,000 members and an attendant staff of administrators, clerks, janitors, engineers, and others may no longer lay claim to the early character of a band of scholars. But the function of the university makes it essential that the faculty—its effectiveness, and the zeal and continuing growth of its members—shall be the central concern of a university's administrators. The characteristics of the faculty— of the roles its members play as individuals, of the training they bring to their tasks, of the views they hold, and of the kind of people they are—constitute an essential part of the context to which administrative process must be adapted.

Role of the Faculty Member

In one day's time, a faculty member may be called upon, in addition to teaching his classes, to speak at a community luncheon, to plan or attend a special conference, to finish the writing of a technical paper, to answer correspondence, and to meet in the afternoon with a faculty committee and in the evening with a student group. Such a varied pattern of demands fractures his time and makes intellectual concentration on teaching and research difficult. Yet the multiplicity of purposes of the institution imposes an obligation on the faculty member to participate in such varied tasks.

The faculty member faces a pervasive uncertainty as to what is expected of him. If he fails, for example, to serve on an *ad hoc* committee or to make a speech as suggested by the dean, will this limit his advancement as a teacher? Yet such services may limit his preparation for teaching or delay the book upon which his promotion or salary increase will rest.

The dean or department head, on the other hand, finds it difficult to meet the demand for other services and, at the same time, provide incentives for effective performance of the primary function of the institution. A private firm, an attorney, and, to a lesser degree, a public servant may refuse to perform the public services or may perform them in return for a foreseen and valuable return. The faculty of a university may see no valuable return but accept the obligation from a sense of professional purpose which overrides personal motivation. The increasingly important role of the highly trained individual in an increasingly complex civilization steadily broadens the external dimensions of the faculty member's role.

The faculty member's roles as teacher, research man and scholar, and communicator all tend to isolate him from other participants in the university organization. The function of the university dictates that each department shall bring in scholars with different backgrounds to teach the specialized courses that make up the curriculum of a broadly equipped university. The individual, in the main, is expected to teach his courses according to his particular bent and background. Hence, the academician carries on his scholarship more in concert with colleagues at other institutions specializing in his field than with colleagues in other departments and schools of the university.

When he faces the public, he does so as a specialist and consultant, sought after for his particular knowledge, and not as a contributor to an organized activity. This contrasts sharply with personnel in business, industry, and government, whose activity rests largely on association with others and participation in group operations. The extent to which the role of the faculty member either requires or encourages "teamwork" [9] deserves patient and thorough analysis. Students of university administration may well consider whether it still makes sense to pretend that the faculty of a multipurpose university is *one* body. If the university is really more an aggregation of relatively discrete parts, what does this mean for governance?

High Degree of Specialization

Recently the new president of a Middle Western college told of his shock in discovering that he was the "only man on the campus concerned with the whole institution." He went on to decry the divisive influence upon faculty members of their intense specialization in particular fields.

In effect, what has happened is that the average faculty member has become during the past 100 years oriented more to his discipline than to his institution.[10] He tends to want to influence and to interpret institutional decisions in terms of their effect upon his discipline, or even upon his particular laboratory, library, or personnel needs. The administrator, in contrast, is forced by his function to

[9] Theodore Caplow and Reece J. McGee, *The Academic Marketplace*, Basic Books, Inc., New York, 1958. In their section on "collaboration and isolation," these authors make clear that, while some collaborative research does take place, there is by and large no concerted effort to encourage group activity within the departments of the institutions they studied.

[10] Around 1940 a college president of very long experience commented, "When I first became a president the *average* professor was a former clergyman attracted to college teaching by his interest in young people; as I retire, the average professor is a subject matter specialist accepting teaching as the price of opportunity to continue his specialized studies."

think more in terms of the institution. The result is a cleavage between the two. The specialized professor tends to question whether administrators can understand his field of specialization adequately to make budgetary and other decisions which affect it. This conflict between "particular" and "universal" outlooks is not unique to the university, but it tends to be more intensive here than in the business firm or the public agency.

This situation encourages the faculty member to set himself up as an individualist committed to resisting intrusion in his area not only by his departmental chairman and deans, but even by his colleagues. He feels that he is the only one who knows the particular problems of his particular field of study. More than this, he may even look upon the institution, in the outspoken words of a physical scientist at one major university, as obligated to support him and his research for the good of society.

This contrasts sharply to the orientation of the "organizational man." William H. Whyte, Jr., has illustrated this distinction in describing the role of the scientist in industry. The scientist, he contends, is: [11]

. . . the direct antithesis of the company oriented man. If the company wants a first-rate man (scientist) it must recognize that his allegiance must always be to his work. For him, organization can only be a vehicle . . . nor is it companionship, or belongingness. What he asks is the freedom to do what he wants to do.

Management has tried to adjust the scientist to the Organization rather than the Organization to the scientist. It can do this with the mediocre and still have a harmonious group. It cannot do it with the brilliant; only freedom will make them harmonious.

The university is not alone in facing this problem of specialization. For example, the Naval Research Laboratory with 1,400 professional persons on its staff or the large laboratory of a private business presents many problems similar to those of a university.[12] Within the university the problem is intensified by the existence on

---

[11] *The Organization Man,* Simon and Schuster, Inc., New York, 1957, p. 201.
[12] William G. Torpey, "The Professional Employee Replies to Management"

its faculty of a greater array of specialists than is found elsewhere. In the university the problem of synthesizing the activity of many self-oriented individuals and of the competing faculties of many departments and several schools becomes the point at which the academic success of an institution is often made or lost.

The individual who has acquired professional status, by dint of long and specialized training, has usually also acquired (or claims) four perquisites of his status: [13]

1. He has a self-contained logic; that is, he persists in the application of intellectual processes that are different from those of the administrator or the businessman.

2. He has ingrained working habits. Because he has been trained to work on his own, he is apt to insist on having complete control of the way he shall do the job.

3. He applies objective standards of performance to his own work instead of accepting the evaluation of a superior.

4. He regards the imposition of conventional personnel practices ". . . as the very antithesis of professional status; and there is nothing that he resents more deeply. Conversely nothing appeals so much to his idea of the status due him as does direct responsibility to work out for himself the personnel practices and procedures that concern him and his group." [14]

The context within which the university operates, hence, imposes on its administration the necessity of adapting, on the one hand, to the faculty members' lack of an institutional perspective, and, on the other hand, to their insistence as professional people to a concern in all decisions that may affect their status as individuals or freedom to pursue their specialty as they deem best. The faculty member often manifests the same "arrogance of the specialist" that is exhibited by the actuary in the insurance company, the geologist in the oil company, or the lawyer in many enterprises. He insists

---

(supplemental to Drucker article noted below), *Personnel Administration,* vol. 17, no. 1, January, 1954.

[13] Based on a discussion by Peter Drucker, "Management and the Professional Employee," *Harvard Business Review,* May, 1958, p. 88.

[14] *Ibid.*

that the administrator accept and be guided by his unquestioned advice in the field of his specialization! The faculty member claims the right to participate in decision making on many other aspects of institutional policy.

Commitment to Values

The professor spends many hours in the logical organization of knowledge and in the search for new and useful facts and concepts. This concentration causes him to strive for systematic schemes or values which aid him in the handling of knowledge. More than his counterpart in other institutions, he is likely to hold as important for organizational decisions such choices as absolutism versus relativism, objectivity versus commitment, freedom versus authority, and sacred versus secular. Hence, a needed decision on a practical matter may be deferred until theoretical issues are debated.

Concern with such fundamental commitments shifts the faculty member's focus away from institutional needs. Thus, recently the faculty of a major Eastern university was unable to decide on a curriculum for a program in public administration because of disagreement on the fundamental role of the state in society. The publicly known views of a professor will enter into his acceptability for service on a university faculty—as in the example of Bertrand Russell and his association with the City College of New York.

The other commitment commonly held by the professor is that he must be free to teach and express the ideas he holds. He vigorously defends his right to pursue his specialized inquiries wherever his intellect leads and to report his findings. This commitment often underlies differences between faculties and external groups and leaves the administrative officer caught between.

Congressional attacks on foundations in recent years have reflected a fear that the scholar who is given freedom to conduct research which "might lead anywhere" will come up with "all sorts of undesirable ideas." Sensitive to any encroachments on the intellectual activity which forms the essential core of his living, the professor resists any possible intrusion.

The Nature of the Professor as a Person

The faculty member, in addition to being a professional man with deep and sensitive intellectual commitments, is a personality conditioned by the environment out of which he has come. The rigorous and extended training in academic institutions which constitutes that environment tends to create, in the view of some observers, a common personality typical of faculty members.

The personality that eventually emerges from all this, George Williams contends,[15]

is typically underlain with a deep sense of inferiority, fear and maladjustment, yet overlain by an almost frantic sense of superiority. This deep split in the personality is further complicated by a latent hostility to that which is nonbookish and nonintellectual, and a fluttery insecurity that creates morbid fear of any criticism that may endanger hard-won academic place.

Harold Stoke writes of three "traits" of the professor which are akin to those pictured by Williams. He writes of: [16]

(1) the peculiar value of job security to faculty members, not only as an adjunct of academic freedom but also as a necessary freedom from personal anxiety. . . . (2) a more trying trait which can develop as an occupational hazard for the college professor is arrogance. This grows out of the easy victories of the classroom where he works with young people who know less than he does. He may thus unconsciously come to believe that business, politics, and educational administration would be much better managed if those in charge would only apply the same intelligence to their work that he uses in his own. . . . (3) . . . the tyrannical nature of the teaching profession, its haunting sense of things undone. During every waking hour the conscientious professor feels driven by his inadequate preparation for teaching, by the books he has not read, the articles not yet written, the ideas not yet clearly formulated. Inside or outside

[15] *Some of My Best Friends Are Professors,* Abelard-Schuman, Inc., Publishers, New York, 1958, p. 50. See also Logan Wilson, *The Academic Man,* Oxford University Press, New York, 1942, pt. 2, pp. 15–96; Henry S. Canby, *Alma Mater; The Gothic Age of the American College,* Farrar & Rinehart, Inc., New York, 1936.

[16] *The American College President,* Harper & Brothers, New York, 1959, pp. 115–116.

the classroom and laboratory he carries this guilty load, and it creates for him a sense of strain and indeed a continuity of labor not adequately reflected in the formal teaching schedule.

These statements offer no precise description of the personality of all college professors. They suggest, however, some of the attitudes and traits which contribute to the context within which universities operate, and with which administrators must cope.

PAUCITY OF RESOURCES

Most American colleges and universities exist in relative poverty. Their earned income meets only a fraction of their annual operating costs. Not more than 10 per cent of all private and public colleges and universities have endowment income sufficient to provide as much as one-fifth of the annual budget. The publicly supported colleges and universities have derived substantial and increasing revenues from appropriations, but not sufficient to raise the "level of living" in most such institutions above the parsimonious level. The funds required to build the classroom buildings, laboratories, and dormitories needed to serve rapidly growing enrollments have been provided with relative generosity by a number of state governments, but are financed with greater difficulty from borrowing or "begging" by the majority of private institutions.

The effect of the relative poverty that constitutes an obvious element of the context within which most institutions operate is especially obvious in the low level of salaries that obtain for faculty members in all except a few of the better-supported private and public agencies. It is reflected, too, in the assistance and facilities available to aid the faculty in their teaching and research. There is less in the way of resources to finance the extracurricular venture than in the analogous business or in most governmental enterprises; the professor who would undertake research requiring funds for travel or for equipment, or the teacher who would take his class off to observe operations integral to the topic being studied, seldom has ready access to the funds needed.

Yet there are evidences that the relative poverty which colleges and universities have long experienced has not influenced major aspects of the educational programs. In many institutions it has not reduced the wide variety of courses that are offered largely because of the interest of individual teachers, not because there is a clear student demand for them. And in many institutions it has not brought about the utilization of classrooms and laboratories for a greater part of the year (more than nine months) or for a greater part of the day (more than from 8 A.M. to 1 or 3 P.M.).

CHARACTERISTICS OF THE INSTITUTION

The university, in its structure and in its functioning, reflects distinctive characteristics which are the inevitable consequence of the functions it performs and of the central staff which constitutes the institution's backbone.

Minutely Segmented by Discipline

The diversity of a university's purposes results in the existence within the university of many departments and schools or colleges. Each is concerned with a single discipline or profession. In addition, there has inevitably grown up a complex and varied array of research institutes, laboratories, hospitals, and special programs, and of administrative offices ranging from those concerned with student personnel services to those concerned with financial and physical plant operations.

It is the basic academic unit, the *department*, that poses problems of coordination that are unique to the college or university.

The departments are more than an administrative convenience, the Macmahon report pointed up succinctly.[17]

They reflect the existence of distinguishable disciplines or assemblages of subject matter; these in turn reflect the past history of scholarly inquiry and the social context in which it has been conducted. Accordingly, the reorganization of disciplines and specialties may be required when the methods of inquiry in a specific area change, when new knowledge opens fresh fields of investigation or rearranges old ones, or when the juncture

---

[17] Macmahon, *loc cit.*

of problems in the world at large calls for a new focus of scholarly interest. At such times the inherited departmental structure must not be allowed to interpose an element of rigidity that works against the advancement of knowledge. A decisive test of the effectiveness of the University's organization is the degree to which it insures a continuing re-examination of the specific departmental structure it has inherited.

The department is, at the same time, an organizational subdivision and an association of individuals with professional ties. The allegiance of its members to the profession or discipline in which they are trained, rather than to the institution as a whole, does reduce the effectiveness of efforts to enlist the enterprise of these individuals in modifying curricula, budgets, and programs as the needs of knowledge and society may dictate. David Riesman has dubbed the departments "the intellectual veto groups" within a university.[18] He has charged that it is frequently the department which impedes the making of decisions that would alter existing curricular arrangements (and indirectly the professional societies associated with each) and dynamically develop the institution's educational program.

American institutions of higher education have devised a variety of devices and methods to overcome the narrow specialization by discipline that is reflected by the departmental structure. Fundamentally, departmentalization is a consequence of research specialization. At Wesleyan and, in an earlier period, at Stanford, divisions [19] were established in an effort to provide a means of interrelating the instruction offered by the departments. At Princeton a number of offices concerned with geographical areas and broad fields of scholarship, e.g., the humanities, are designed to attract the interest of individuals from several disciplines. In other institutions seminars are used to bring together teachers from different fields.

Further complicating the administrative process, however, is the fact that most institutions of higher education present two struc-

[18] *Constraint and Variety in American Education*, University of Nebraska Press, Lincoln, Nebr., 1956, pp. 53–106.

[19] Divisions have existed at Harvard since the 1890s and at the University of Chicago since 1931.

tural arrangements operating to a large degree on a parallel basis. One involves the "line" relationships emanating from the president and relating the heads of various offices and deans and departmental chairmen in a scalar pattern. The other is formed by the various faculty legislative bodies primarily concerned with educational policy and emanating from the faculties of individual departments upward to institution-wide councils or a "senate" or meetings of the total faculty. The latter groups in some institutions have direct access on occasion to governing boards, as well as to presidents. Presidents, indeed, usually serve and "chair" committees of the university senate. In this way the two lines of power reassociate with the president to provide a nexus of both lines of power.

The problem for decision making is the determination of connective tissues to unite these parallel structures into an operating whole. At the same time, whatever arrangements are used must be sufficient to stimulate, not to thwart, the enterprise of the individual faculty member as a creative teacher and scholar.

What organizational mechanisms tend to enlist the enterprise of faculty members to the ends of the institution? What policies can gain cooperative support of individualistic, specialized faculty members when organizational structure supports rather than inhibits their independence? To what extent is this diverse structure essential for enterprise in relationship to the importance of unified participation in the organization?

These and related questions deserve exploration. They promise to yield findings of real significance in counteracting the divisive and handicapping effect of the diversity of purposes reflected by the departmental structure.

Influence of External Groups

Another characteristic of the university to which structure and administrative process must be adapted is the substantial interest and influence of those groups which *create* colleges and universities (e.g., the state or church authorities), which *support* them (e.g., the state, the church, alumni, and others), and which *preserve* them (e.g., the constituencies and alumni).

For every type of organization there are external but related groups whose support or contribution is essential to the continued functioning of the entity. For example, a manufacturer of jet engines usually depends upon a wide variety of suppliers to produce the various components needed. If the required quality of production and the agreed-upon schedule are to be assured, the services of these subcontractors must be effectively integrated. Similarly the manufacturer's structure and practice may be influenced by investment bankers and by important customers. Much the same situation exists for a governmental bureau. A unit of the U.S. Department of Agriculture, e.g., the Forest Service, may adapt its structure and processes to serve the lumber, recreational, and grazing interests it serves. Indeed, it must adjust to their wishes or be confronted with substantial opposition when seeking congressional support.

So in the college or university, the allegiance of external groups (alumni, professional constituencies, parents, prospective donors, and public and church bodies) is necessary for continued existence. The nature of the bonds with these groups varies considerably from that of suppliers and bankers to commercial enterprise or the constituencies to public agencies. So do the extent and variety of the pressures these outside groups exert on decision making by individuals within the institution. Hence, the adjustments in structure and in practice that are made to mobilize, maintain, and control the interests of such groups by the college or university constitute a unique, even if similar, element in the governance of these institutions.

The distinctiveness of the relationships between external groups and educational institutions lies in two elements. One reflects the variety and number of interested outside groups and their tendency to apply pressure, without accepting a commensurate obligation to support or to contribute. Although alumni, parents' groups, accrediting associations, professional bodies, and others require colleges and universities for their existence as organizations, they are not dependent upon any one higher institution, nor are their individual members usually dependent upon them for a livelihood as in

the case of the subcontractors for the manufacturer of jet engines.[20]
The other arises from the intimacy with which members of these
outside groups operate in the decision-making councils. The institution of the American college alumni hardly needs emphasis. In
the words of Robert G. Sproul, president of the University of
California, they "never cease to think of themselves as members of
the family." [21] Nearly every university or college as well has a small
number of interested outsiders who provide substantial financial
support and in return assume an intimate relationship with the institution, oftentimes as trustees. The bond of parents of undergraduates to the urban college or university is minor, but shows evidence
of broadening and deepening. A measure of their interest is reflected
in the fact that over $4 million was given by parents in 1956 to
all colleges and universities.[22] Such groups as these have a close
relationship to the decision-making process; in the case of alumni,
this relationship is formalized in alumni councils and similar bodies,
and by alumni membership on boards of trustees.

The extent of control by other groups is broad. Pressure groups
of national and local character attempt to exercise influence on the
character of the educational program. Accrediting associations and
professional bodies such as the chemical and engineering societies
set standards for both programs and staff. State legislatures and
other bodies providing public support establish many operating
rules and frequently exercise financial, procurement, and legal con-

[20] Colleges and universities are frequently under fire from various pressure
groups and public bodies (such as congressional committees) for the actions or
statements of individual faculty members outside of the institution itself. Thus,
in a recent election, a college in the New York City area found itself under bitter
attack from a local Republican political "boss" because members of its faculty
worked for the Democratic organization. No similar attack was made on business,
industrial, or other organizations for the personal political actions of their
personnel.

[21] Quoted in an article by Theodore A. Distler, "Responsibilities of Alumni
for Quality in Education," 1955 Yearbook, American Alumni Council, Washington, part 1.

[22] Educational Fund Raising, 1956 Annual Fund Survey, American Alumni
Council, Washington.

trols over day-to-day functioning.[23] At times they influence internal action through the functioning of citizens' advisory bodies. The sponsorship of research by both private and public agencies influences the kind of research and scholarship carried on.

Decision making, therefore, takes place under the pressure of external forces which have more direct and powerful influence than the customer-supplier-company or public-bureau relationships of other institutions. In addition, such groups, by their own representative (as suggested above) and through the allegiance of faculty members to their professions and disciplines, frequently operate within the decision-making councils in a manner not demonstrated in other institutions.[24]

The Right of Professors to Indefinite Future

Tenure, in the final analysis, is derived from the principle of academic freedom and owes its existence to social, not individual, advantages. It is an element of administrative practice which grows naturally out of the responsibility of the university to society as well as the needs of its faculty. It is secondarily the recognition of proved capability in the form of a guarantee of indefinite employment. In large corporations unwritten policy frequently will assure executive and white-collar workers who possess seniority another place in the organization before outright dismissal. A method similar to that of universities and colleges is effective in many law firms, where permanency of status is recognized by granting a kind of tenure as a junior or senior member of the firm. Similarly, some management consultant firms recognize a successful and extended apprenticeship by advancement to the rank of "principal" or "partner" which carries permanency as a member of the group.

Obviously, the assurance of tenure provides recognition for the organizational member of a demonstrated ability. Less fortunately,

[23] See Malcolm Moos and Francis E. Rourke, *The Campus and the State,* Johns Hopkins Press, Baltimore, 1959, especially chaps. 3–7, pp. 43–181.

[24] For example, when he insists upon certain facilities and staff requirements, the head of the department of chemistry may in fact reflect the interests and objectives of the American Chemical Society rather than the interests of the institution which employs him.

it protects those members who use it as the basis for slowing down their contributions or resisting policies of the organization. This problem has gained recognition in business and government. It has special importance in educational institutions. There, a relatively large proportion of all participants are on tenure, and this fact enhances an already existent tendency toward the personal independence that is inherent in the professional and specialized status of faculty members.

On the other hand, tenure in higher institutions assumes a very special importance by assuring to the individual the freedom to be intellectually creative, by furnishing protection against those who would disagree with him and bend him not only to institutional but also to outside pressures. The nonconformist represents an administrative problem in all kinds of organization, but the non-conformist (and there are too few of them) also reflects a creativeness that is most important for intellectual leadership.

What educational administrators face is the need for—and the problem of—accompanying the protection afforded by tenure policies with arrangements which stimulate the growth of the professor.

Tradition of Administrative Autonomy

Closely allied with the specialization of the faculty member and the "building-block" character of the department in the organization of the university is the relative autonomy granted the department. Presidents and deans find it difficult to direct or evaluate the work of departments and their specialist members. Take, for example, the position of the president of Stanford University when he is confronted with the proposal of his physics department that he seek $10 million or more from the government to build the linear accelerator that the President of the United States subsequently endorsed. He is little able to evaluate the proposal himself. He may have among his deans or personal assistants an individual with the specialized competence required to evaluate the proposal, but the odds are that he will be dependent upon the recommendations of the physics department. Decision concerning course requirements by a curriculum committee offers another (and more common) example. Technical questions may be raised that most members do not understand, and reliance is placed upon the recommendation of the department supporting the proposal.

This situation plus administrative tradition results in an administrative process that grants more and more autonomy over their special areas to the academic departments and schools. Governing boards rely upon recommendations from presidents; presidents upon deans; deans upon departmental chairmen. The department and the professional school have achieved decisive influence, because their recommendations for staffing, course requirements, and other academic policies are increasingly difficult for nonspecialists to evaluate.

To a lesser degree this situation develops in any expanding enterprise. But business organizations have an effective base line in productivity or profit, church organizations in a common agreement on purposes, governmental bureaus in a legislatively and publicly approved budget. In universities, the autonomy of the department and school is increased and reinforced by the need for diversity, the subject-matter orientation of faculty members, and the tenure essential to the academic freedom and security of the teacher.

Thus, we find the Association of Collegiate Schools of Business, in support of institutional departments, insisting upon administrative separateness for accreditation. The law school at one major Western university, not untypically, insists that its autonomous status requires not only administrative recognition but a separate building. The insistence of schools and departments upon having separate and specialized libraries raises questions not only about the efficiency and effectiveness of library administration but also about the availability of books to all students without expensive duplication.

As the demands on universities to educate a growing body of students push ahead of resources, the organizational autonomy accorded schools and departments poses increasingly difficult questions. Few administrators advocate intrusion into the intellectual arena of the department. But many find the achievement of coordination and operational efficiency difficult in the face of the high degree of autonomy that prevails in the college or university.

SUMMARY AND AVENUES FOR ADVANCE

Because of the force of tradition and custom, it is folly to seek precise processes and procedures to meet the administrative problems with which universities are being confronted as they steadily grow larger. What is needed is clearer recognition of the distinctive characteristics of the university as an administrative enterprise. In spite of the fact that universities have existed for centuries, little has been written that aids the administrator or the student to identify the respects in which the university differs from the business firm, the military, or the public organization as an administrative enterprise.

It is this task to which the foregoing pages have been devoted. More thorough analysis is needed to ensure that each of the distinctive characteristics which affect administration has been identified and that, having been identified, its real significance is ascertained. Before we can design better organizations and conceive better administrative processes and practices, we must understand fully the context within which the university operates.

The studies of institutions, large and small, which have preceded the drafting of this volume have revealed that those characteristics which together constitute the context of university administration can be identified. Their influence on the governance of universities will be suggested if inquiries are made into:

The Appropriate Roles of Major Participants in the Governing Process

It is high time that objective and thorough analysis be directed toward the respective roles of the trustees, the presidents, the deans, the department heads, and the faculties.

The Decision-making Process

There is a substantial opportunity to shed light on the problems of governing in colleges and universities if the processes by which decisions are arrived at are subjected to effective comparative analysis. This means a comparative consideration of the elements of decision making—planning, communicating, appraising—in business, governmental, and university enterprises.

The College or University as a Social Institution

In the end the several participants in the governing process and the techniques they use should be viewed as a whole. Perhaps studies of universities and their total effectiveness as human enterprises may be the most fruitful way of revealing means of improvement.

It is along these three avenues that succeeding chapters will seek to advance the understanding of the influence of context on administrative practice.

Chapter 3

ROLES OF UNIVERSITY-WIDE OFFICERS

ORGANIZATIONAL DUALISM

THE ADMINISTRATION of institutions of higher education presents a unique dualism in organizational structure. Most American colleges and universities distribute the work of "deciding" and "doing" according to conventional scalar arrangements.[1] Most have a president (or chancellor) and an administrative staff, which usually includes an academic dean or provost and officers for the areas of finance, student affairs, physical plant, and alumni and public relations, as well as deans of major instructional or research units and chairmen of departments.

Paralleling this scalar organization, each college and university has a traditional structure for the formulation of faculty decisions with respect to a broad range of educational problems and such other matters as may be entrusted to or are a matter of interest to the faculty. The faculty of each department, either as a group, acting formally or informally, or through its chairman, recommends or

---

[1] See James D. Mooney, *The Principles of Organization*, rev. ed., Harper & Brothers, 1947, p. 14. "The scalar principle is the same form in organization that is sometimes called hierarchical . . . it means the grading of duties . . . according to degrees of authority and corresponding responsibility."

decides policies affecting this unit. Similarly, the faculties of each school or college within the university decide or express their views, as a body or through a network of committees, on a variety of matters. A similar organizational structure obtains on an institution-wide scale for the expression of the general faculty will.

RATIONALIZING THE DUALISM

Theoretically this dual organization is rationalized by the fact that both the administrative hierarchy and the successive echelons of faculty governing bodies operate on the basis of authority delegated by governing boards. Alexander Brody, in a survey of historical and contemporary relations between universities and state governments,[2] has made an excellent study of the "flow of authority" in institutions. The essential point made by Brody and by Elliott, Chambers, and Ashbrook [3] is that the governing board legally is the institution—with powers to enact rules and regulations, to engage and discharge faculty members and administrative staff, to charge tuition and fees, and to maintain discipline. The essential assumption to rationalize this organizational dichotomy is that the delegations made to these parallel organizational structures are clear and mutually exclusive.

Under charters granted by state governments and charter laws, colleges and universities have come into being by the legal establishment of governing boards with authority to organize the institution, administer it, and maintain it for posterity.

As W. H. Cowley states succinctly, governing boards are created by the public, are granted authority to organize and administer the institution by the public, and are responsible for maintaining it in the public good:

The problem of relations (administration versus faculty) grows out of the fact that about four centuries ago the paramountcy of the civil

[2] *The American State and Higher Education,* American Council on Education, Washington, 1935.

[3] E. C. Elliott, M. M. Chambers, and W. A. Ashbrook, *The Government of Higher Education,* American Book Company, New York, 1935.

state became clear. Thus, it developed that all other kinds of government could exist only with the approval of civil government. In short, the civil government made "concessions" to other governments to perform certain social functions. These "concessions" were made in the form of patents or what we today commonly call charters . . . instruments licensing the recipients to perform specified activities.[4]

The authority of governing boards has been markedly reduced since the days when board members personally examined all graduating seniors. The expanding size of institutions has forced the same delegation of authority to subordinate officers as has characterized the evolution of commercial and industrial organizations. Much authority has been delegated to the president in practically all institutions, and as the size of the institution increases, the delegation to administrative officers and to deans and departmental chairmen tends to be greater. Yet there is little evidence that a carefully thought-out design underlies the delegation pattern that obtains. Rather, prevailing organizational arrangements suggest that the existing patterns of delegated authority have been established to meet specific situations in particular institutions or to reflect the strengths and weaknesses of individuals in various echelons.

Much of the authority of governing boards has simultaneously been delegated to—or been claimed by—the paralleled faculty organization. Several forces have combined to bring about this result. The failure or inability of governing boards during the past century to take the lead in formulating educational policy has created a power vacuum. Their delinquency has given rise to one of the most provocative contributions of recent decades to planning for higher education, i.e., Ruml and Morrison's *Memo to a Trustee*.[5] Similarly, the trustees' contribution in practice to the selection and evaluation of faculty members has been largely a rubber-stamp approval of faculty proposals.[6]

[4] Unpublished lectures at the University of Illinois, 1959.

[5] Beardsley Ruml and Donald H. Morrison, *Memo to a College Trustee,* McGraw-Hill Book Company, Inc., New York, 1959.

[6] See, for example, Charles P. Dennison, *Faculty Rights and Obligations in Eight Independent Liberal Arts Colleges,* Teachers College, Columbia University,

Faculties, by and large, have sought a larger role in decision making related to educational and faculty policy. Together these forces —the incapacity of governing boards and the ambitions of faculties —have accounted for the large and increasing control that the faculties have gained over educational policy.

Tradition constitutes a third—and most important—force that has resulted in giving the faculties substantial responsibility for educational decisions. This responsibility is formally established in the bylaws of many governing boards or in faculty statutes the boards have approved. The tradition that the faculty, a body of scholars, should have autonomous authority over educational matters has grown out of the customs and practices of English, German, and other Continental universities. Indeed, European professors who visit this country often evidence surprise that lay outsiders and nonscholar administrators should presume to exercise power over educational affairs.

As with the scalar organization, a panoramic view of the authority exercised by the faculties—at the institutional, the school, and the departmental level—reveals no consistent pattern of delegation. Comparative analyses of the functioning of faculties in a number of institutions show wide variations in the matters with which faculties deal. These analyses also reveal marked differences in the ways in which responsibility for the formulation of faculty views or the making of decisions is distributed among the departmental faculties, the school faculties, and the general faculty. Variety is a preeminent characteristic of American colleges and universities, and that characteristic is clearly reflected in the ways in which they organize to give expression to faculty views.

New York, 1955; and Theodore Caplow and Reece J. McGee, *The Academic Marketplace*, Basic Books, Inc., New York, 1958. Caplow and McGee report (p. 183) that in their study of the filling of professional vacancies and replacements in ten major universities during the academic years 1954–1955 and 1955–1956, they discovered no instances "in which the governing board of any university refused to approve a candidacy or turned down a recommendation for appointment."

DECISION MAKING IN ACADEMIA

That the process of decision making in the university or college has distinctive features was pointed out on page 10. The purpose of this chapter is to examine the roles played in academic governance by officers of the university who are concerned with the whole institution: the board members and the president. Chapters 4 and 5 will consider the authority for decision making delegated (formally, by chance, or by tradition) to the academic officers, i.e., the deans and department heads, and to the faculty or faculties.

Within the past two decades students of administration have recognized that the process of decision making is at the heart of the administration of any enterprise.[7] Moreover, their analyses have demonstrated that decisions are not in practice individual, authoritarian actions.[8] Decisions result from the interaction of individuals and groups, the general administrative or institutional "climate of opinion," the various attitudes which those persons involved in the process hold, and the environment in which the enterprise operates.

In its simple form decision making involves a number of factors which can be combined into three general steps: the definition of the issue and the investigation necessary to understand it; the consideration of the alternate possibilities and the consequences of each; and finally the choice or action to be followed.[9] While the final choice among alternatives may be made by one person, the choice may really have been determined by many other individuals who participated in the course of the steps that led up to the final decision.

[7] See particularly Herbert A. Simon, *Administrative Behavior*, The Macmillan Company, New York, 1947.

[8] Mary Parker Follett, writing in the late 1920s on "The Illusion of Final Responsibility," said, "An executive decision is only a moment in a process. The growth of a decision, the accumulation of authority, not the final step, is what we need most to study." In Henry C. Metcalf and L. Urwick, *Dynamic Administration*, Harper & Brothers, New York, 1940, p. 146.

[9] See, for example, the writings of Edward H. Litchfield, Herbert A. Simon, Chester Barnard, and Luther Gulick.

In a small college, for example, the president may make a decision on the location of a new building by collecting various opinions and necessary information from all persons within the institution who are concerned (such as faculty members, departmental chairmen, the comptroller, and the superintendent of buildings and grounds) and from outside specialists (such as architects and builders). Upon the basis of this information (frequently at a meeting with the leading administrators), he examines the consequences of various locations, applies his values to the facts in making a choice among alternatives, and then makes his recommendation to the trustees. Trustees (for purposes of our example) approve his recommendation.

In this instance, then, the president was the key figure in the decision; others shared in the process, and indeed the architect or superintendent of buildings and grounds may have effectively decided the matter for him. That he sought their views or relied on their advice makes him none the less a strong executive; rather it reflects his capacity for utilizing his staff. Although the board approved his choice and formally made the decision, in reality the decision was an institutional action.

It is in this sense that we are concerned with the roles in governance that boards, presidents, deans, chairmen, and faculties play in college and university administrative operation. This chapter will be limited to an examination of the roles of trustees and the president in each of the principal functional areas in which decisions have to be made, i.e., academic affairs, faculty selection, promotion and compensation, student affairs, finance (current and capital), physical facilities, and public and alumni affairs. This chapter will explore how the unique structural characteristics of most colleges or universities facilitate or impede trustees and presidents in decision making. Theirs is the responsibility for making decisions which will ensure that the institution over which they preside is to meet the evolving demands of the society within which it exists. And theirs is the responsibility for harnessing the opinions and the will of all members of the institution that decisions may be wisely made and vigorously executed.

THE ROLE OF THE TRUSTEES

THE PROBLEM FACING GOVERNING BOARDS

The broad authority of governing boards caused Samuel P. Capen, former chancellor of the University of Buffalo, to declare that they constitute a "simon pure example of authoritarian government." They are endowed with broad powers. Morton A. Rauh has pointed out that, "In most cases the enabling charter or legislation gives the board full power to manage the institution." [10] And Ruml and Morrison, after asserting that trustees have final responsibility and authority for the performance of their institutions, declare that ". . . they may abdicate from their position of authority, but they cannot annul it; they may vacate their posts, but they cannot destroy them; they may delegate activities and decisions but they cannot thereby avoid their own responsibilities." [11] And despite their broad authority, seldom are they required to account to any higher authority for their stewardship.

At the same time board members find themselves (1) dependent on others for the formulation and effective making of many decisions for which they are ultimately responsible, (2) inadequately informed about the basic operations for which their institution exists, and (3) unable to influence decisions that determine the basic character of the institution as an educational enterprise for which they (influenced by tradition) have delegated authority to the faculty.

On the one side, boards have such powers as those provided by the statutes of the State of Ohio for the trustees of Ohio State University. "The Board of Trustees," the statutes state, "shall elect and fix the compensation of and remove the president and such number of professors, teachers, and other employees as may be deemed

[10] *College and University Trusteeship*, The Antioch Press, Yellow Springs, Ohio, 1959, p. 13.
[11] *Op. cit.*, pp. 3–4.

necessary. The Board shall fix and regulate the course of instruction
and prescribe the extent and character of experiments to be made
at the University." [12]

On the other side, one distinguished university president reflects
the views of many board members when he states that in the three
universities in which he has served, the trustees were consistently
dissatisfied with their position, not feeling that they had an effective
or substantial part to play. In less complaining terms, the Paley
report (Columbia University) [13] points up the need of the typical
governing board for fuller understanding of the central educational
operations over which it presides. This report eloquently reflects
the groping for a satisfying definition of function that typifies the
thinking of many other board members.

EVIDENCES OF BOARD FUNCTIONING

What place, then, does the governing board have in the decision-
making processes of American colleges and universities?

Clues to the place the board has in decision making can be
found only in the actual functioning of boards, i.e., in such
tangible evidences of their functioning as the frequency with which
meetings are held, the committees used to carry out their functions,
and especially the record of matters considered and of documents
available to the boards on which actions were based. Obviously
these manifestations of board action do not reveal the influence
that trustees exercise. They offer only a factual and limited picture
of the part played, not of the influence exercised.

Number of Meetings

Eight of the ten boards studied meet four to six times each year. [14]
One board meets monthly and one annually; most of their business

[12] Ohio General Code, sec. 7949.

[13] *The Role of the Trustees of Columbia University,* report of the special
trustees committee adopted by the trustees, Nov. 4, 1957.

[14] In a study of the activities of presidents of state universities Ila D. Weeks
found that two-thirds of 46 state university boards met 9 or fewer times a
year; one-third met 6 or fewer times each year. *National Association of State
Universities Transactions and Proceedings,* 1950, p. 20.

is handled by committees. Meetings, therefore, tend to be formal affairs for official approval of matters previously worked out by the president, the board chairman, and committees. As a rule, significant decision making does not occur at official board meetings, particularly by the larger boards. At Georgetown University [15] members of the board are also administrative officers, so that the board does consider a great deal of the administrative and educational policy of the university. However, in this instance, ultimate authority lies with the Jesuit order. The order appoints the president, who in turn serves as the chief executive.

Committees

The majority of boards operate through an executive or similar committee which keeps in active communication with the president and serves for the board between regular meetings. As the membership of its board would indicate, Georgetown University does not have an executive committee, in this sense, because the board itself can meet regularly. In most instances, particularly for private institutions with large boards, the executive committee in effect serves for the board, which officially approves its recommendations or actions at regularly scheduled meetings. In some instances (e.g., Sweet Briar College), separate boards of "directors" and of "overseers" essentially perform these two roles.

Usually, boards will have two or three other important committees whose recommendations in effect are the decisions of the board. Thus, at the University of Toledo, the former board committees on financial affairs and on general administration (superseded in 1958 by a single executive committee) met separately at lunch during the week before board meetings to formulate the decisions that would be approved at the board's formal meeting.

---

[15] The organizational structure of Georgetown University differs markedly from the pattern of governance prevailing in non-Catholic universities. In lieu of an outside lay board of control having full legal and formal authority over the institution, there is a board of directors composed of 11 Jesuits. The only appointed member of this board is the rector (president). The remaining board members are officers who serve on the board by virtue of their position in the university. Others may be added by consent of the board members.

At Stanford, similarly, the board committees meet prior to the monthly board meeting. In each institution approval of the recommendations of the committees at the official board meeting is customary and becomes largely a routine matter. (At Toledo, action is taken in committees primarily in order to keep discussion of controversial matters from the press, whose representatives can attend official board meetings.)

Three types of committee are common to each institution surveyed (except Georgetown University). These are the committees on finance or budget or, in some instances, audit; on investment, endowments, or gifts and grants; and on physical plant or buildings and grounds. This and other evidences suggest that these three areas comprise the bulk of all decision making for many governing boards.

On the other hand, the extent of the participation by boards in the making of educational decisions, i.e., in matters of degree requirements, curricula, and courses, was early suggested by the conclusions of Elliott et al.[16] They indicated that only 6 per cent of the governing boards of 91 institutions surveyed had committees concerned with academic policies. Moreover, the records of current meetings of a number of boards, e.g., at Cornell, Minnesota, Virginia, Stanford, and others, indicate that faculty members seldom appear before the board. At Denison and Wesleyan universities—both rather small, private institutions with strong traditional liberal arts background—on the other hand, the governing boards have committees concerned with the educational program and apparently exercise a fuller interest in educational policies. At Princeton a joint trustee-faculty committee regularly meets to discuss developing educational programs.

Matters Considered

Records of board meetings reflect very directly the committee structure. Agendas and business consummated, other than formal approval of presidential recommendations on educational policy and personnel appointments, show a primary concern with budgets

[16] *Op. cit.*, p. 121.

and financial policies, investments and endowments or other special incomes, and the development of the institution's physical plant and properties. Except at Georgetown, Denison, and Wesleyan, the records of board meetings reflect consideration of relatively few educational matters and the routine approval of faculty personnel actions.

WHAT ARE THEIR RESPONSIBILITIES?

The foregoing evidences of governing boards' activities do not state their responsibilities. Numerous views on what responsibilities trustees should have can be found, but among them much difference of opinion obtains, especially in one major area.

The Paley report summarily states that: [17]

The major legal responsibilities which devolve upon the trustees are:

(a) To select and appoint the president of the university;

(b) To be finally responsible for the acquisition, conservation, and management of the university's funds and properties;

(c) To oversee and approve the kind of education offered by the university, and make certain that its quality meets the highest standards possible.

Selecting a President

There is general agreement that the most important single responsibility of the governing board is the selection of a new president.[18] It is, however, a responsibility that never confronts many trustees, and those who are called upon to perform it do so with little experience. Yet in this task they discharge a responsibility that influences every aspect of the functioning of the institution for a period of years.

An analysis of the manner in which three university boards—

[17] *Op. cit.*, p. 20.

[18] Ray J. Quinlan, chairman, Board of Regents, University of Minnesota, in an address before the Association of Governing Boards, Dec. 1, 1953. See also Barnaby C. Keeney, "The Function of the President as Interpreted in the *Memo*," *Journal of Higher Education*, 30:426–431, November, 1959, p. 431.

Princeton, Toledo, and Virginia—selected presidents during 1959 offers significant reflections on how such decisions are made.

1. Each board formulated an explicit or implicit statement about the kind of individual they sought. In two institutions the lay board members clearly indicated that they sought a scholar (preferably from their own institution) and manifested little concern with prior administrative experience. In one institution, Toledo, the board squarely stated that it wanted an educational administrator, i.e., an individual trained as a scholar who had had administrative experience as a departmental chairman, as a dean, as the president of another institution, or in a similar position. There they obtained a man with substantial administrative experience.

2. Each board followed a simple procedure in seeking nominees for the post. The alumni were politely invited to offer suggestions. The faculty's views were invited in two institutions. Foundation officers and executors of educational associations were visited and their suggestions solicited. Many other university presidents, e.g., Henry M. Wriston and Harold W. Dodds, were canvassed by letter or telephone. Lay board members, lacking familiarity with personnel in other institutions, sought widely the advice of professionals in the field, on whom they relied for the evaluation of men whose skills in the educational field they were not adequately equipped to appraise.

3. The part the faculty was invited to play in two institutions— Princeton and Virginia—was a large one; in Toledo the faculty was accorded little or no part. In the former institutions committees of the faculty assisted the boards at the start in formulating criteria for the kind of men wanted. They recommended men for the boards' consideration, and reviewed and commented on other individuals whose names were brought to the boards' attention.

Acquisition, Conservation, and Management of Funds

There is no question about the responsibility of trustees for the finances of the institution. Faculty, academic and administrative officers, the president, alumni, and students all look to the trustees to ensure that there are resources with which to pay adequate salaries to faculty members and to provide essential libraries, laboratories, and equipment.[19] And trustees that work at their jobs readily accept this responsibility.

The governing boards, however, in making—or, more exactly, in approving—decisions about finance and about the development of the institution's physical plant and properties, do influence significantly activities on which there is less agreement that they should have any responsibility. The annual budget is in effect a fiscal statement of the institution's educational program. By setting salary levels for the faculty, the board influences the caliber of the educational offering. In determining what physical facilities shall be provided, in choosing between laboratories and dormitories, a student union building and a classroom building, the board similarly influences the educational program.

Overseeing and Approving Educational Program

It is about the third responsibility stated above that differences of opinion prevail. These differences are effectively illustrated by the debate that has been provoked by Beardsley Ruml. This author contends that the board of trustees is finally responsible, under the institution's charter, for the educational program as well as for the property of its institution, and that it is accountable for the institution's performance to the state, to the national and local community, to donors of property, to parents and students, and to the faculty. And this author has brought down on his head the wrath of academic people generally by arguing that the trustees should "take back from the faculty as a body its present authority over the design and administration of the curriculum." [20] Ruml argues that the trustees must "take back" the responsibility for design and administration of the curriculum "not because the trustees, *as a board*, are able to exercise it better than can the faculty as a body," but because the board "does have the final authority and accountability."

Opponents of this view contend that trustees cannot and should

[19] See address of Victor S. Bryant before the Faculty Club of the University of North Carolina at Chapel Hill, Oct. 2, 1956.
[20] In Ruml and Morrison, *op. cit.*, p. 13.

not take a direct part in the educational process "because they do not know how to do so." [21] Those who hold this view essentially believe that the trustees should select a president and a faculty, delegate responsibility for the educational program to the faculty, and then concentrate on finding the resources needed to support the program the faculty establishes.

Between the Ruml-Morrison point of view and the opposing view a more meaningful (and desirable) role for the trustees has been described by a wise and experienced layman who has had much experience with education as a trustee and in other capacities. Laird Bell, former chairman of the Board of Trustees of the University of Chicago, has declared that trustees normally join these boards because they are interested in education, and they resent "being told to keep hands off the most interesting part of the activity. . . ." Indeed, he argues, "trustees cannot abdicate *all* concern with educational matters." They "have the right—and in fact the duty—to determine what kind of education shall be offered. . . . But once overall policy is decided it *ought* to be true that the educational experts should determine how the policy is to be implemented. . . ." [22]

Moreover, as laymen giving laymen's views on educational matters, board members can serve a useful purpose. President emeritus Harold W. Dodds of Princeton contends that trustees usually like to hear about educational matters, and enjoy hearing faculty members describe their plans and progress (when the administration takes the trouble to set up the meetings properly).[23] Without infringing upon the proper discretion of the faculty, Dodds declares, board members accomplish a great deal by asking intelligent lay questions. Thus, they ensure thorough thinking out of the proposals that are presented for approval, and their effective interrelation with financial, personnel, public relations, and other considera-

[21] Keeney, *loc. cit.*

[22] "From the Trustees' Corner," *Association of American Colleges Bulletin* 42:353–361, October, 1956.

[23] At Princeton a "curriculum committee" of the trustees meets quarterly with representatives of the faculty to discuss the plans and proposals for changes and improvements in educational program.

tions. It is only when board members forget they are laymen (except for those who are professional educators themselves) that they really begin to meddle.[24]

Protecting Public Relations

Charles Coolidge, a distinguished senior member of the Harvard Corporation, has emphasized an additional responsibility of the governing board. It is the continued protection and promotion of the institution's public relations.

In the institutions studied, the boards sometimes had to show support publicly for actions the institution had taken. Two instances, for example, involved the vigor with which university officials had disciplined students for public misbehavior. In two other instances the board publicly defended the president's action in dismissing professors. In still another instance the board defended one of the schools of the university against criticism for accepting a grant from a much criticized foundation.

Each of these instances affirmed Mr. Coolidge's emphasis on the trustees' obligation and singular ability to aid with public relations. Here were instances in which only the distinguished representatives of the public who serve on the board could speak to defend the institution.

CENTRAL PROBLEMS FOR TRUSTEES

The Paley report at Columbia has outlined two critical areas in which research on how to make boards more effective will be most useful. The first is in the development of improved techniques of communication between faculty and board. The problem is how to keep the board informed about the central educational problems and programs of the university, while assuring that the board will not substitute its untutored judgment for the judgments of educators on educational questions.

The second problem is in the clearer definition of the responsibility of the governing boards. It is idle to say that all authority

[24] In a letter to the author, Jan. 13, 1959.

flows from the board. In fact, analyses of their decision making indicate clearly that they do not presume to extend their authority over *all* questions that arise in the operation of a college or university. Moreover, analyses of the membership of boards raise questions as to whether the members bring to their tasks capacity or experience enabling them to decide fundamental questions of educational program, or to select the faculty. A rationale for the part the board should play in these central areas of decision making is needed.

A third problem of large significance may be stated in these words: What responsibility should trustees assume for interpreting to the faculty the evolving needs of the society from which they come and for impelling the faculty to consider how courses and curricula should evolve to equip students to enter this evolving society? This is not to suggest that board members are always more accurately sensitive to or even aware of the evolving needs of society than are historians, economists, sociologists, or political scientists. It is to suggest that board members should be able to light up angles of the problem not apparent to the professors and to provide an additional, more comprehensive and pragmatic interpretation of society's course.

Available evidence suggests that few governing boards and few individual trustees perform this role. Should they? If they do not, how are the pragmatic over-all needs of society and the realistic views of lay leaders in the society forced into the educational programing of the institution?

THE ROLE OF THE PRESIDENT

DISTINGUISHING FACT FROM FICTION

In assessing the role of the modern-day university president, the primary task is to distinguish fact from fiction. The stereotype of the university president in the minds of many within the academic community, and a greater proportion without, is of a distinguished educator exercising large, independent, and unchallenged authority in the management of the institution over which he presides. The historians and analysts of our institutions of higher education, and the biographers of their presidents, have, by and large, painted a picture of a distinguished statesman with great power,[25] active in the affairs of his day, and accomplished educator giving leadership to his faculty, and a revered guardian of his students.[26]

Yet observation of their day-to-day activities poses a contrasting picture of modern-day university presidents. A lifelike picture is afforded by analyses of how the time of university presidents is spent. Ila D. Weeks, president of The State University of South Dakota, devoted his presidential address in 1950 to a discussion of replies from his colleagues in the National Association of State Universities. He had asked each of the state university presidents to complete a questionnaire describing his relations with his faculties, students governing boards, alumni, legislators, and the general public; and the activities, in connection with each, that take his time. Dr. Weeks's summary of their replies is an informative, factual picture of what consumes their time.[27] A briefer, similar description of the role of the modern university president is offered by the results of analyses of how the time of two major university presidents (one in a large state university, the other in a major, but smaller, private university) is spent. In summary these men, on the average, devote approximately:

40 per cent of their time to financial matters: framing the budget, presenting it to trustees and to the legislature, reviewing with advisers the management of invested endowments, and especially appealing to prospective donors.

[25] Most recently Paul F. Lazarsfeld and Wagner Thielens, Jr., in *The Academic Mind*, write of the "great power" of the president. Free Press, Glencoe, Ill., 1958, p. 178.

[26] Harold Dodds, former president of Princeton University, contends that there is still "much of the Mr. Chips in the stereotype held by the American public of the university president."

[27] Ila D. Weeks, "The University President and the Publics," presidential address, *National Association of State Universities Transactions and Proceedings*, 1950, pp. 12–25.

20 per cent to public and alumni relations: meeting with, and usually addressing, a variety of public, alumni, and parent groups, including state and national educational associations; writing for alumni publications and working with the alumni secretary; participating in service club or church activities or service on corporate boards of directors.

12 per cent to problems of physical facilities: developing plans for needed classrooms, buildings, laboratories, dormitories, and other facilities with either legislative committees or the donors providing needed funds.

10 per cent to general administration: dealing with university business officers, and meeting with board committees to consider such problems as the management of dormitories; the maintenance of grounds and buildings; the procurement of supplies; the treatment of clerical, custodial, and other nonacademic employees; or the problems of the university press.

18 per cent (less than one-fifth) to educational matters: meeting with faculty representatives or otherwise working on matters of educational programing; meeting prospective new faculty members; selecting and promoting faculty members, department heads, and deans; meeting with student groups and student leaders and handling, with his staff, student problems, including those arising out of the fraternities, and especially out of intercollegiate athletics.

Obviously such quantitative approximations offer no precise depiction of what the presidents do. Least of all do they depict the role he may wish to play in institutional governance; indeed, his wishes little influence what he actually does, for, as Barnaby C. Keeney has written, "the president himself must be responsible for whatever is going badly. If education is going badly, he must devote almost his whole time to education. If the dining halls are going badly, he must concern himself primarily with them." [28]

The foregoing summary analyses of how two university presidents spend their time do not reveal a statesman, educator, and modern-day Mr. Chips or Mark Hopkins. Rather they depict the university president as an executive concerned predominantly with financial matters, public relations, physical facilities, and other

[28] Op. cit.

administrative affairs. They picture the university president as spending less than one-fifth of his time working on educational matters and keeping in touch with his faculty or with his students.

The role played in the governance of their institutions by the presidents of smaller institutions studied may vary markedly from that pictured above. Butterfield at Wesleyan devotes less time to financial matters, to public relations, to problems of physical facilities, and to administrative affairs; he spends a major portion of his time on faculty recruitment and evaluation, on educational programing, and on direct contacts with student groups. The presidents of Beloit, Denison, and Goucher similarly give more of their time to internal educational, faculty, and student affairs; but in each instance the problems of finance and of public relations claim a large portion of their time. The president of Beloit, after devoting much of the first year or two of his incumbency to working with his faculty on curricular, faculty-building, and student relations problems, felt impelled to concentrate his time on the development of the institution's financial resources. The president of Denison devotes a major share of his time to public and alumni relations. The demands placed upon the president of Goucher by the movement of the campus from downtown to the suburbs markedly limited, for a period of years, the time he could give to other matters.

In short, observation of the day-to-day functioning of typical college or university presidents suggests that as the institution grows in enrollment, and hence in faculty, in facilities, and in budget, the president is ejected from the areas of the institution's central concerns—the educational program, the faculty, and the students—by the demands that are made on his time by other activities.

ROLE IN EDUCATIONAL PROGRAMING

So far has this trend gone that one respected state university president has declared that neither he nor any other large university

62   GOVERNANCE OF COLLEGES AND UNIVERSITIES

president has any major part in the educational programing of his institution. The suggestion that educational leadership is one of the president's functions is labeled "novel," perhaps facetiously, by Barnaby C. Keeney, president of Brown University.[29] Yet many observers of the university presidency vigorously contend that the primary role of a president is "educational leadership." For example, J. Douglas Brown, dean of the faculty, Princeton University, writes that "The president of a liberal arts college (or a university) . . . should be the first member of the faculty, and essentially its leader in general educational policy." [30]

Customarily the president presides over the university senate, or an analogous body, and is frequently an ex officio member of its principal committee and of the faculties of each individual school. Demands on his time preclude his regular participation in each of these bodies and prevent most presidents from taking the lead in discussions relative to courses, curricula, and programs.

It is usually the well-established and exceptional president, such as Butterfield of Wesleyan, Dodds of Princeton, or Sterling of Stanford, who can lead his faculty in introducing educational advance. Yet, there are notable exceptions to this generalization. Eliot at Harvard, Arthur Morgan at Antioch, and Aydelotte at Swarthmore can each be said to have provoked educational change as they strove to establish themselves as presidents. Yet the experience of Alderman of Virginia is more typical. He wrote that he waited five years after his inauguration before presuming to suggest any innovations in the institution's educational program. His successor, Darden, was sharply rebuffed when he appeared before the faculty to argue for a proposed degree program. And one university president, best unnamed, who moved rapidly after his inauguration to effect educational program changes, commented to the author: "A faculty seeks

[29] Op. cit., p. 428; for stimulating suggestions about the president's role, see David Riesman, "Planning in Higher Education: Some Notes on Patterns and Problems," Human Organization, 18(1):12–16, 1959.

[30] J. Douglas Brown, "Mr. Ruml's Memo: A Wrong Approach to the Right Problem," Journal of Higher Education, 30:412–416, November, 1959, p. 415.

you out to serve as president because you have ideas, and then 'cuts your throat' if you venture to promote the adoption of such ideas." Practically, presidents do exercise much influence over the character of their institution's educational program through their control and use of the budget. By giving support here and denying it there, the president can, if he will, frame the educational character of the institution. But it is a sad commentary upon the role of the American university president that he must achieve such educational change as he can through indirect financial levers. In practice he is seldom either the author of big, new ideas about educational program or the stimulus that evokes such ideas from others, nor is he often permitted to participate in the give and take of faculty discussion of educational program proposals. There are college and university presidents who are in fact the educational leaders in their institutions; their number is small.

ROLE IN FACULTY SELECTION

The president (and his principal academic officer—provost or dean of faculties) devotes relatively little time to matters of faculty selection. This generalization holds true despite the existence of notable instances in which the president does play a prominent part.[31] He has few opportunities to initiate the selection of professors. He often plays a *negative* role by questioning proposals for appointments; and some presidents insist upon interviewing individuals whom they are asked to recommend for tenure appointments. More often, however, he influences the selection of faculty through his selection of deans, and sometimes department heads, and by working with them to ensure agreement on high standards for faculty membership.

[31] This view contradicts the view offered by Caplow and McGee, *op. cit.*, p. 184, to wit: "the president and vice president also play a formalized and passive role in the recruiting process." On the other hand, James B. Conant, in his final report as president of Harvard University, when looking back over his years of service as president chose to emphasize his role in faculty selection.

ROLE IN STUDENT AFFAIRS

A frequent complaint of the university president is that he has too little time to devote to student affairs, and to coming to know individual students. Other matters consume his time so fully that he is no longer a "master" of his students in the traditional educational sense. By and large, decisions on matters arising out of student academic affairs, e.g., control over absences, remain in the faculty; while decisions on student nonacademic affairs, e.g., discipline, fraternity affairs, and recreational affairs, are made by a dean of students in the larger institutions, or by the faculty as a body in the smaller institutions. The dean of students is the president's man; his activities are under the continuing surveillance—and influence—of, or at least are the responsibility of, the president.

The president becomes personally involved in deciding questions relative to the students and their nonacademic life usually in four instances. Matters of athletics are of such large public and alumni consequence that the president is forced to give personal attention to such questions as membership in an intercollegiate athletic conference or the hiring of a football coach. Flagrant infractions of discipline by students, particularly those involving drinking and relations between the sexes, usually demand presidential participation. Ideological issues posed by students—the inviting of a controversial figure to the campus, the presentation of views in student publications that differ markedly with prevailing economic and social views—similarly require presidential attention. Finally, his attention is called for in some instances when students are demanding an enlargement of their own responsibility for governance.

In short, the decision-making role of the president in student affairs is usually small, but is often large when the going gets rough, for the final responsibility is his. He delegates responsibility for governance of student affairs to the dean of students, with the knowledge that the faculty continually oversees this officer's actions. His own participation in this area of decision making, except in times of emergency, is precluded by other demands on his time.

ROLE IN FINANCE

In contrast, the president is with few exceptions the central figure in deciding questions relating to the current and long-run financing of the institution. He may delegate much responsibility to deans, department heads, the provost, or his vice president for finance, but he is usually assigned formal responsibility for preparing the annual budget and presenting it for approval to the governing board. In the public institution he must, in addition, present the budget to the legislative body and gain its sympathetic consideration. In the private institution, he must plan and lead the perennial or continual campaign for financial contributions from the alumni and from the public.

Two factors limit the president's ability to utilize the budget as a means to modify or formulate the institution's educational program. First, the institutional expenditures are relatively inflexible; a large proportion of all expenditures are for fixed costs: the salaries of the tenure faculty and the maintenance expenses of the institution. Second, the balance between available revenues and essential expenses is so close that the president has little free money (except in unusually well-to-do institutions). The resources needed to undertake a new educational program or with which to launch a new enterprise of any sort are seldom available except when tuition is raised or an unexpected bequest is received.

The president's influence over the budget is further limited by the concern on the one hand of the faculty, and on the other of the trustees with this central instrument of governance. Relatively few faculties, as a body, play any substantial, formal role in budget formulation.[32] At Minnesota, where a senior faculty committee reviews the budget with the president each biennium before it is submitted to the legislature, the action is exceptional. More often the deans are given an opportunity to present estimates of their needs; and while department heads and faculties have an opportunity to

---

[32] Notable among the exceptions of which the author is aware are the University of Illinois, Oberlin College, and Reed College.

make their demands, entreaties, or urgings, they have no decisive part to play. The trustees, or more often a committee of them, take a more active, and in some instances a commanding, position in determining what shall be included in the budget. At George Washington University, for example, the finance committee "hears" the heads of each school or college justify their budgets and has a major part in determining the annual budget.

It is still the president and his chief financial (or development) aide who bear the brunt of obtaining the resources needed either from the legislature or from donors. And in this manner he materially influences the eventual decision. Yet here the influence is that of the office of the presidency more often than of the man; most presidents work in close concert with a financial officer—vice president, treasurer, or comptroller—and this officer, usually a close, trusted aide, may exercise substantial influence over the institution's fund-raising program.

ROLE IN DEVELOPING PHYSICAL FACILITIES

The hallmark of the president's office in American universities is a large plan to scale of the campus, showing the new buildings planned or for which funds are sought. And it is not the unusual president who may appear at a faculty committee meeting or a cocktail party with mud stains on the cuffs of his trousers, having just tramped through the rising foundations of a new building.

In deciding which among the several needs of the institution— library, dormitory, laboratory, classroom building, or athletic field house—is to be given priority, the president will usually have a principal influence. He may consult with a faculty committee. He will be pressured by his aides—the librarian, the deans, or the director of athletics. He may be strongly influenced by prospective donors, or less often, in the public institution, by the legislative committee. And he must gain the approval of the trustees. But the final, formal decision will usually be his.

Once it has been determined that a building shall be built—and many such determinations must be made in the governance of a university—the decisions that must ensue may be made by others. The president can entrust many subsequent decisions to his vice president for business affairs, to his comptroller, to his director of planning, or to his superintendent of buildings and grounds. But he will likely have to insist upon being continually consulted and informed about the details of design and construction so that he, in turn, may satisfy the interests of the trustees (or a committee of trustees) or of a donor.

ROLE IN PUBLIC AND ALUMNI RELATIONS

The president is inevitably the spokesman for the institution. He is the vehicle through which routine announcements are made about the dates of scheduled functions, the addition of courses or curricula, the appointment of faculty members, the acceptance of grants and gifts, and a myriad of other actions. To assist him in this activity he will usually have a director of public information, publicity director, or director of press relations. With the aid of this assistant he decides what university-wide announcements shall be made and in what terms; and he reviews some or all of the announcements that are made by the deans and others for their respective schools or divisions.

A greater proportion of his time is devoted to the making of speeches before selected groups.[33] Through the statements he makes before public, educational, and alumni groups, he determines, in significant part, the posture that the institution shall have in the minds of important constituencies. These statements constitute, in terms of the influence they exercise over important supporters, as well as in terms of their indirect influence on the thinking of faculty and staff, a far more significant element in the governance of the institution than is recognized by most observers of the presidential role.

[33] Ila D. Weeks, *op. cit.*, found that of 46 state university presidents, 13 presidents reported that they made 50 or more speeches each year.

RESPONSIBILITIES ARE SHARED

In each of the areas of decision making that have been depicted, the president shares in greater or lesser degree both the opportunity and the responsibility for decision making. He shares with the faculty the opportunity to make decisions about educational program and faculty selections. He can influence decisions in each of these important areas, but few presidents are allowed to initiate educational change or faculty selections directly. He has formal authority to approve, but the positive element of decision making— the formulation of the decision—he can, in practice, influence only through tactful persuasion.

In the development of educational program it might be wished that the president could play a role similar to that Dean Acheson once envisioned for the Secretary of State in the formulation of foreign policy: [34]

The formulation of judgment as to facts, probabilities, policy and actions calls for an institutional effort . . . for the sweep of the matters which should go into the making of most judgments is so vast, they are so interrelated and complex, require such depth of particularized knowledge, and call for such syntheses that no single mind or small group of minds is adequate. . . . The organized and disciplined work of many highly trained minds is necessary.

Assuredly these words apply almost without modification to the formulation of modern educational curricula and the need for the views of many members of a faculty. Moreover, Acheson writes eloquently of the ideal relationship of the president to his faculty when in analogy he writes: [35]

The Secretary wants and needs their [the professional staff of the Department of State was in Acheson's time as large as the faculties of most large universities] inspired best, and it is he who must evoke it. He must be their protector and inspirer, their critic, the appreciator of excellence, harsh toward shoddiness or conclusions contrived to comply with currently accepted notions. He cannot be aloof. He must share and guide

[34] *The Atlantic Monthly*, December, 1953.
[35] *Ibid.*

their thought, partake of their perplexities. He must give as well as receive. His mind must enter into their minds, and theirs into his, so that the product of their common work is advice which the government of this nation can wisely and practically put into execution in the world as it is.

For the words following *common work* substitute "is the establishment of educational curricula attuned to the evolving demands of a society and incorporating all that is known of the advancing technology of teaching and of each emerging field of knowledge." The statement as reframed offers an effective description of the ideal role of the president of the liberal arts college, or even of the larger multipurpose university.

He has a greater measure of independence in deciding questions arising out of student life (usually through his aide, the dean of students) but here he shares responsibility with the faculty (and perhaps alumni) on the increasingly important matter of admissions and on questions of intercollegiate athletics.

His scope for independent decision making grows larger in the areas of finance, physical facilities, and public relations. Yet his decisions on annual budgets, proposals to the legislature, or annual fund-raising campaigns are regularly reviewed by the trustees. These are matters with which the trustees "feel more at home" and on which their aid may be required. Hence, the intensity of their appraisal of the president's decisions is greater, and their insistence upon participation in the decision is greater. Few faculties insist upon having an opportunity to voice their views on the annual budget and on the relative priority of building needs. But the faculty does not expect to exercise an influence over these matters comparable to the influence they claim over educational programing and faculty selection.

COMPREHENSIVE RESPONSIBILITY AND LIMITED ROLE

Wandering through time, one can uncover concepts of leadership expressible in such different terms as *patriarch, master workman, captain, dictator, inspirer,* and *diplomat-persuader.* The history of institutions of higher education in America indicates that leaders describable by each term have served as college or university presidents. But which is the model for the modern college president? The president's responsibility is as comprehensive as the institution's concerns, but the authority he is permitted to exercise over academic governance is far more limited than is popularly supposed. The president who exercises large influence over the governance of his institution, especially in the educational areas, does so by dint of consultation, persuasion, and suggestion. He may reinforce his suggestions by the decisions he makes in each annual budget, but even while making these decisions, he will be seeking funds to finance, in most instances, educational activities he is striving to change.

He is, as other observers have noted, the center of power in his institution. Indeed, his role may be graphically suggested by the accompanying chart. He has a part in the making of decisions in

ROLE OF THE PRESIDENT

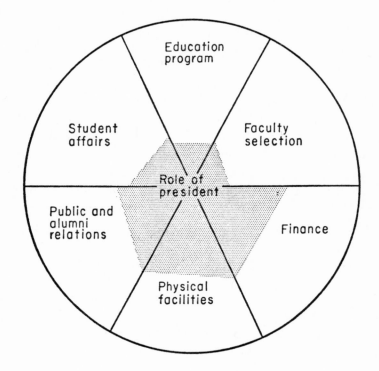

each principal area of governance. But in each area he is opposed by countervailing forces—the faculty, the trustees, the students, the alumni, or other constituencies. The extent of his influence varies markedly in each area in accordance with his ability to cope with these forces. The profile of the governance role of a typical president is suggested by the darkened center portion of the chart.

The central problem in the university president's role in governance, and one with which students of university administration may well concern themselves, is hence: How does the president extend his influence over decisions that affect the central purpose of the institution, i.e., educational programing and faculty selection, to which he (and his immediate aides) alone can contribute a university-wide viewpoint to balance the views of a dean, a department head, a committee, or a faculty member concerned with a parochial objective? What traits of personality or administrative skills are required to enable him to extend his influence in these areas?

Chapter 4

ROLES OF THE ACADEMIC OFFICERS

THE GROWTH in size and complexity of the college and university has made the tasks of administration increasingly difficult. The growth in enrollments not only has brought to the institutions greater numbers to educate, but has brought an increasing proportion seeking, for vocational ends, a range of courses not previously offered. Larger enrollments require larger faculties, and the increased number of teachers constitutes another force for the introduction of a widening range of courses—in their specialties. Larger faculties have found it increasingly difficult—or impossible—to conduct much of the educational "business" of the institution in faculty meetings. Thus, the faculty as an all-institutional body has tended to disappear or to be inane.

Together these forces have placed a heavier burden upon the central academic leadership of the institution. To cope with this burden, the apparent tendency has been for the president to turn over first to deans, and then to department heads, increasing responsibilities for academic decision making. Hence, in this chapter the roles played by these academic officers—deans and department heads—in the governance of American colleges and universities in the late 1950s are examined.

72

THE ROLE OF DEANS

THERE ARE MANY KINDS OF DEANS

Former Dean Herbert E. Hawkes of Columbia College commented, "There is no such thing as a standardized dean. There is a dean of this and that college, but I never have seen any two deans who could exchange places and retain the same duties." [1]

Dean Hawkes might have added: "There is a dean of this or that activity." For, in addition to deans of colleges, there are found "deans of students," "deans of men," "deans of women," "deans of social sciences" (and of other subject-matter groupings), "deans of faculties," "deans of summer schools," "deans of extension work," and still others.

In short, a wide variety of offices bear the title of dean. They fall into six general categories: (1) those with responsibilities for the whole institution, titled dean of faculty, dean of the university, dean of academic affairs, or even provost; (2) deans of students or dean of men and dean of women; (3) deans of arts and science colleges, including those of units within a university and of separate liberal arts colleges (sometimes under the title "dean of faculty"); (4) deans of professional schools and colleges; (5) deans of graduate studies; and (6) deans of evening and extension divisions.

Here we are concerned with the last four categories. The deans concerned with the whole institution (category listed first above) and deans of students (category 2) are excluded from this consideration on the grounds that they usually are, except in the largest institutions, a part of the office of the president. They serve as university-wide officers supplementing the president, and aiding him with the business, financial, public relations, student living, recreational, and morale problems, and other noneducational activities of the whole institution. The other categories of deans, with which we

[1] H. E. Hawkes, "College Administration," *Journal of Higher Education,* 1:245–253, May, 1930, p. 245.

are concerned here, focus a larger share of their time and energy on educational matters—curriculum, faculty selection and promotion, student admissions, discipline, and related affairs—and a lesser portion on financial, business, public relations, and other noneducational affairs.

HOW THE DEAN'S ROLE HAS EMERGED

The dean's role in the governance of the American college or university has emerged from two sources. On the one hand, the office of dean came into existence with the establishment of separate and relatively independent professional schools. The first American deans, W. H. Cowley has reported, appeared early in the nineteenth century. On the other hand, the position of dean has been established in many institutions to aid the president and to take over, principally, educational functions which the president can no longer perform. This was a principal reason for the establishment of the office of dean of Harvard College in 1870. Since that early date, in many other institutions the president, forced by expanding demands on his time, has delegated more and more responsibilities to his dean or deans.

This emergence of the dean continues. To assess the role of those three categories of academic deans—(1) of the colleges of arts and sciences; (2) of the professional schools and colleges; and (3) of the graduate, evening, and extension divisions—is to draw a bead on a moving target. The processes of delegation of responsibility, on the one hand, from the faculty, and on the other hand, and more substantially, from the president, continue. These processes of delegation are observable in small institutions and in large; but the rate at which delegation proceeds increases substantially as the size of the institution, and especially the size of its faculty, grows.

Hence, one can assess the part in governance of the dean only by (1) considering separately the roles of the three categories of deans listed above, and (2) identifying the part played by each in each of the major areas of decision making: educational program; faculty selection, promotion, and development; student affairs; finance;

development of physical facilities; and public and alumni relations. In short, it is impossible to identify the role of "the dean." It is possible only to describe the functions performed in each of these areas of decision making by deans of each type in institutions of various sizes.

THE ROLE OF DEANS OF ARTS AND SCIENCES

The deans of arts and sciences colleges—in small liberal arts schools, in the larger colleges (e.g., 1,000 to 1,500 enrollment), and in many universities—generally have little responsibility for the long-term financing,[2] the acquisition of needed physical facilities, or the alumni or public relations of the colleges over which they preside. There are significant exceptions to this generalization, especially in the largest private universities, but by and large the dean is not expected to bear these responsibilities. In many instances, the dean may be called upon to talk with prospective donors; to aid in campaigning for a new library, dormitories, or classroom buildings; or to meet with alumni or public groups. Indeed, in none of the fifteen institutions studied is the dean of arts and sciences held responsible for formulating financial, building, or public relations programs or for the accomplishment of such programs.

Role in Smaller Colleges

In many smaller institutions the dean devotes a principal part of his time to handling student affairs. He is burdened down with the tasks of judging excuses for class cuts; rectifying registration entanglements; keeping a variety of records; writing to parents; counseling students on academic, personal, and financial affairs; writing letters of recommendation; and handling an assortment of correspondence not warranting the attention of the president.[3]

[2] There are notable exceptions. In 1959, the dean of the faculty at Princeton University traveled approximately 30,000 miles to meet with alumni groups throughout the United States and to advance the "$53 million campaign" to support the building of new facilities and to strengthen the teaching and research programs.

[3] Mary Frances, "The Office of the Dean of Studies," in R. J. Deferrari (ed.),

His role, in the smaller college, in the selection and in the promotion and fixing of compensation of the faculty is, in effect, as assistant to the president. He may, and the most effective deans do, play a constructive role in assessing the capabilities of the faculty, field by field (there will be few departments of considerable size in a faculty of 30 to 80 members), and in searching for able instructors and assistants to bring in as vacancies permit. The magnitude of his role, and of his influence over the institution's decision making in these areas, depends in principal part upon the president. The president may, and if the dean is a strong able person, often does, delegate much to the dean. Or the president may insist upon deciding questions about faculty selection, promotion, and compensation himself, especially in the smaller colleges.

The dean's responsibilities for leading the faculty in a persistent reexamination of curricula, in order to adapt courses and programs creatively to the changing requirements of the society for which students are being trained, tend to be small. Pragmatically the extent of his responsibilities is a consequence of (1) the time the president has left over after attending to fund raising, public relations, and administrative affairs; and (2) the nature of the president's personal interests, be they fundamentally educational or administrative. More often than not in the small colleges the president manifests an inherent interest in educational programing and clings to the control of this function. Because the educational program consumes a major part of the college's budget, the president controls most curricular and faculty decisions and markedly limits the role played by the dean.

Role in Larger Institutions

As the institution grows larger, the dean customarily is relieved of many or most of his responsibilities for student affairs. The dean of students takes over responsibility for student counseling, and for most contacts with parents and with employers.[4] The registrar as-

---

College Organization and Administration, The Catholic University of America Press, Washington, D.C., 1947, pp. 85ff.

[4] The role of the dean of students in the administrative organization of a uni-

sumes the record-keeping tasks. The director (sometimes dean) of admissions takes over the nettlesome problems of student selection. In multischool institutions, particularly those in which there are several undergraduate colleges, these officers will be responsible to the president's office, reporting immediately to the provost, to a vice president for academic affairs, or to a dean of faculties. In the large college they may report to the dean, and his influence may be increased by his control over these activities, even while he has a dean of students to see that the work is done.

The influence and status of the dean tends to grow as the institution grows larger. This is due, in substantial part, to the increased responsibility that the dean assumes for budgeting the funds to be available for the several departments, and for the promotion and selection of faculty members. The "strong" dean will vigorously and tactfully press his departmental faculties to search extensively for the best of talent to fill vacancies on the faculty. Such deans will rigorously insist that departmental faculties demonstrate that the individuals they would appoint or promote to tenure positions are better qualified than men available from other sources. His decision-making authority will usually be limited by one of two arrangements. In some institutions a faculty committee (usually made up of quite senior members) will be authorized to review and express a judgment on new appointments and promotions to tenure rank (e.g., Princeton, Stanford); in other institutions the president will insist upon personally meeting the individual under consideration and forming a judgment on his adequacy (e.g., Cornell, Virginia).

The dean's ability effectively to perform this essential personnel task is usually—not always—limited by the lack of effective method

---

versity and the relation of student personnel work to the institution's goals are eloquently and perceptively discussed by T. R. McConnell of the University of California in "The Relation of Institutional Goals and Organization of the Administration of Student Personnel Work," in Martin L. Snoke (ed.), *Approaches to the Study of Administration in Student Personnel Work*, Minnesota Studies in Student Personnel Work, no. 9, University of Minnesota Press, Minneapolis, 1960, pp. 19–35.

for appraising the individual teacher's performance.[5] Occasional
reports from students, from colleagues, or from the registrar and
evidence on the individual's social acceptability are hardly reliable
measures on which the deans can base their judgments.[6] Yet there
is little evidence that many deans are striving to establish better
measures. Rather the deans observed in the course of this study, with
notable exceptions, cling to the desire "to teach at least one course,"
little realizing the nature of added duties they have assumed as academic administrators. In addition, their time is consumed by the
counseling of students and by a mass of routine administrative action. They have little time for the broad reading that would enable
them to counsel intelligently the representatives of the many departments over whom they preside, stimulate their development,
and participate effectively in educational programing with others
on the faculty.[7]

For, as the institution grows larger, the responsibility for educational leadership devolves on the dean. The president cannot, while
carrying a multiplicity of other duties and while being responsible
for a number of colleges within the institution, give more than occasional educational leadership to the faculty of any one college—

[5] Dr. Louis Benezet stated in a paper read at the 1953 meeting of the Higher
Education Association that:
"1. In the college setting we are making little progress in valid methods for
determining whether or not a given teacher is doing a good job.
"2. We are making little progress in helping young teachers systematically become better teachers.
"3. We are making some progress, but not a whole lot, in persuading older staff
members to consider means by which they can improve those considerable teaching skills they already possess."
[6] Arthur F. Engelbert, "The Professor Looks at the Dean," *The Educational
Record*, October, 1957.
[7] Chancellor Lawrence A. Kimpton, in his 1959 report to the faculties of the
University of Chicago, wrote that ". . . a good dean is a very pleasant thing to
have around, but he shares the weakness of the head of the institution—he rarely
knows what is going on." We attribute this weakness to the tendency to devote
his time to the wrong things; Kimpton attributes it to another and, we believe,
an additional factor, i.e., that he is too little "directly confronted by the
faculty."

or unfortunately, in many instances, even to the dean. The test of the dean often comes in his ability to provide the progressive leadership that is needed, often in opposition to the will of strong departmental chairmen who strive for independence and autonomy. And there are some academic deans who measure up to the opportunity and the function that is theirs, who regularly meet with and stimulate the departmental faculties, who press successfully for building up the membership of weak departments (and there always are some), and who bring members of departments together in fruitful exploration of opportunities for interdepartmental teaching and research, and in consideration of the students' and society's needs.

The difficulty of the dean's position is suggested by the facetious remarks of a long-time faculty member in a large institution (California): [8]

First, everybody wants a firm dean, a strong man. The president will want a famous one, but the die is now cast except for inevitable glorification. A dean must be prepared to state clearly some strong policies and to follow them, come what may. There are one or two odd points about this, in spite of the large amount of agreement. For instance, the desire for a strong dean on the part of many members of every faculty indicates their belief that the one they have is a weak one—which means that he does not pursue their pet causes relentlessly. Investigation discloses the further nature of this paradox. The policies of this strong dean must be his own, else he is not strong, but they must also agree with the policies of each speaker. This is awkward, since no two men on the faculty agree as to desirable policies. The dean who starts out with strong and avowed policies, therefore, is inevitably moderately young, a bit naïve, and recently appointed. However, we must have a good firm strong dean; we will have no namby-pamby type.

Sometimes weak deans are indeed namby-pamby, because usually, of a love of social life, golf, or strong drink. More often they are not namby-pamby but are or become expedient, which is different but has the same effect.

[8] M. S. Marshall, "How to Be a Dean," *AAUP Bulletin*, 42:636–643, December, 1956, p. 638 (professor of microbiology, University of California Medical Center).

THE ROLE OF DEANS OF PROFESSIONAL SCHOOLS

The professional school dean has at the same time a simpler, more complex, and different task than does the dean of the college of arts and sciences in the same institution.

His role is simpler in that he usually has to deal with a smaller faculty. He can often claim a more comprehensive understanding of the several disciplines represented in the faculty. Moreover, the school over which he presides has a greater unity of purpose than the undergraduate college that is simultaneously offering a "broad general education"; preparation for law, for medicine, and for various graduate school specialties; training for teaching; and courses in business techniques. With smaller faculties, and more closely knit organizations, the dean of the professional school (except in the very largest schools) functions simultaneously as dean and department head.

When departments do exist in professional schools, these units usually lack some of the diversity and high degrees of specialization common to the humanities, social sciences, and natural sciences. Professional deans can make (or at the least participate in) decisions affecting most of their disciplines with far greater insights than their liberal arts counterparts. Many professional schools have been organized more recently so that the headship retains much of the status and many of the prerogatives of departmental chairmen. Most professional school faculty members hold the same professional allegiances (as in the areas of law, engineering, medicine, pharmacy, forestry, etc.). This contributes to the relatively close-knit relationship that enables the dean to exercise a greater leadership in educational programing, faculty selection, and budgeting.

His role is made more complex and difficult by a variety of demands which arise from outside commitments. Consulting obligations (which may be the analogue of library research for the arts and sciences teacher); efforts to raise funds for buildings, for faculty salaries, and for scholarships; contacts with prospective employers to facilitate student placement; contacts with professional groups, e.g., the bar association or the medical society; and similar responsibilities fall upon professional deans—in contrast to their liberal arts colleagues. Thus, at Cornell and at Minnesota, as elsewhere, the professional school deans find such responsibilities. The deans of agriculture in many institutions illustrate the multiplicity—the essentiality—of meeting such demands. These deans must build support among the agricultural constituency if the institution is to grow and influence the life of the state it serves.

THE ROLE OF DEANS OF GRADUATE, EVENING, AND EXTENSION DIVISIONS

These academic officers have in common a leadership function to coordinate and develop special educational areas without the aid of faculties serving these areas exclusively. Members of the graduate school faculty are often physically and intellectually affiliated with their respective disciplines—anthropology to sociology—and not with a graduate school staff. Members of the evening school faculty are predominantly part-time evening workers who devote only a few hours each week to their teaching duties. Consequently the roles of these two deans—graduate and extension divisions—differ markedly from those of the deans of arts and sciences or of professional schools.

Some evening school deans have definite educational units with budgets and authority to employ instructors and formulate their own programs.[9] With few exceptions, however, evening and extension deans head divisions for which educational programing and the essential development of faculties are not performed by the individual departments of the institution. These deans rely on the departments for assignment of instructors; and their divisions offer the degrees approved by the regular (usually day and campus) faculty of their institutions. The role of these deans is essentially

[9] At the University of Cincinnati, for example, the Evening College offers its own degree and maintains special educational requirements. The total faculty serves on a part-time basis. The great majority of instructors are drawn from the departments of the rest of the university and are compensated on an hourly basis.

an administrative one. Their time and energies are consumed by the problems of attracting sufficient students, scheduling classes, managing registration, budgeting the division's finances, and arranging for essential physical facilities (e.g., classrooms), books, and equipment. They have little time and frequently little zeal for stimulating the institution's faculty in the teaching and educational planning of evening instruction.

The graduate dean is similar in that he must cultivate an educational area without direct authority for a specific faculty.[10] He is usually, however, an educator at heart rather than an administrator. He enjoys a greater prestige and status, as does graduate study. He may chair a faculty which meets as a body and in committees, but its members hold primary allegiance to their respective departments. Hence, he must develop graduate educational programs through departmental chairmen and faculty committees for graduate studies over whom he has only indirect influence. He often finds it difficult to give substance to the concept of a "graduate school" when graduate students concentrate their studies in one of the subject departments, and the departments regard the advanced students and the graduate classes they offer as "theirs."

His accomplishment is measured in terms of admission standards, of degree requirements, and of the caliber of the faculty. Yet he has little direct influence over any one of these three factors. Standards of admission and degree requirements are established by decisions of graduate faculties as a body or in committees; and the faculty is chosen, in principal part, by the departments. He has an intangible and difficult task requiring great skill at the persuasion of scholars. He has, also, a great opportunity for service, for the building of a great graduate school will bring esteem to the institution.[11]

[10] Exceptions to this exist. At Columbia University, the graduate faculties include political science, philosophy, and pure science. However, graduate professional schools do not come under the dean of graduate faculties.

[11] See, for example, Hayward Keniston, "Graduate Study in the Humanities," a report for the Educational Survey of the University of Pennsylvania, December, 1957; and an earlier study by Raymond M. Hughes, *A Study of the Graduate Schools of America,* 1925.

No attempt is made here to duplicate other analyses of alternative methods of organizing graduate study in American institutions. The sole end here is to appraise the role played by most graduate deans. That role is a coordinative one, with limited opportunity for decision making that significantly influences the total educational program and less the composition of the faculty.[12] Experience suggests that imaginative educational leadership on an institution-wide basis results in greater academic progress than when educational programs are developed by individual colleges, schools, departments, or divisions. Thus, the deans of evening, extension, and graduate divisions are looked to to develop programs through units over which they lack direct control. They gain their ends by patience, tact, and tenacity. They strive to coordinate units that have limited common concern. They face the distressing inertia of departmental noncooperation reinforced by the unwillingness or inability of presidential offices to provide essential support.

QUESTIONS FOR FURTHER STUDY

Several questions suggest profitable areas for further study of the role of deans.

1. In smaller colleges where the president is involved in most areas of decision making, what substantive function is there for the dean to perform? What division of responsibilities between president and dean should obtain?

2. In the larger institution where the president must look to the dean of the college of arts and sciences to supplement his (the president's) own leadership, how does the dean influence educational programing and faculty development? What are his relationships, on the one hand, to departmental chairmen in this connection and, on the other, to the president?

3. To what extent can the dean of a professional school be con-

---

[12] A notable exception is the role played by successive deans of the graduate school at the University of Minnesota. There the dean exercises considerable influence over what members of the faculty may offer courses for graduate credit, and he administers the distribution of some funds to faculty members to support their research.

cerned with fund raising, stimulating the employment of graduates, fostering the support of the professional constituency, and maintaining counseling relationships *and* at the same time stimulate educational advance and faculty growth? Does the typical professional school dean tend to become so absorbed in financial matters, relationships with the school's constituency, and external affairs as to lose influence over educational programing and faculty selection? Does he become so much a "president" that he needs a principal assistant (or dean) to give leadership within the school for educational programing?

4. How and by whom is a dean selected in practice? Is the manner of selection related to the role he plays? And what do faculties (as distinguished from presidents, vice presidents, or provosts) want deans to do?

Underlying such questions is a more basic question. For each college or university—or for higher education in general—what should be the basic administrative unit? Should presidents rely upon the departments of their liberal arts colleagues for the initiative and final controlling of educational affairs?

In recent years, higher education has felt much pressure—most of it not very effective—to integrate the specialized disciplines into fewer, larger areas of knowledge. This has become especially significant at the undergraduate level, where students are expected to have a fairly broad grasp of knowledge in general to supplement their major field of study. Does this pose a similar possibility for administrative organization? If such integration ultimately will have effect, can it be achieved without a parallel structural integration?

Observation of the functioning of deans in many institutions suggests that their role and influence tend to be directly, but inversely, related to the status and power of departments and departmental chairmen.[13] Too little attention has been devoted to the large importance in the governance of colleges and universities of

[13] A self-survey committee at the University of Minnesota has indicated that the dean presents the last line of defense in protecting the integrity of the university's educational program. It intimated that the dean represented the only level from which leadership for his respective unit could come. The president and his staff can do nothing more than give a cursory review of recommendations

the department and its chairman. Hence, we turn now to a consideration of the role of the departmental chairman.

THE ROLE OF DEPARTMENTAL CHAIRMEN

THE POSITION OF THE DEPARTMENT

College and university administrative relationships etch, much more sharply than do those in industry or in government, the limitations of the decision-making authority of executives, who must develop the willingness of the heads and members of subordinate organizational subdivisions to accept their leadership. In the last analysis, authority rests, as writers on administrative theory have repeatedly demonstrated,[14] on the ability of the executive to gain the consent and the concurrence of those he would lead.

Within the larger college and within the university, where departments constitute major organizational subdivisions, this problem becomes one of prime importance for three reasons.

1. Ever-increasing diversity has created an increasing number of organizational subdivisions, i.e., departments. The history of the last hundred years in higher education is one of expanding decentralization. Departments have been created, schools have been formed, as the initiative has come from each subject-matter discipline or professional field. The growth has come not from institutional leadership so much as from the need to satisfy the requirements of individual areas of teaching and scholarship and of growing professional fields.

Decentralized organization with a consequent autonomy among its constituent units has come without the homogeneity of unified policies and purposes. Indeed, the problem is made more complex by the substantial question whether all of the subdivisions of the

---

made by deans. Unless deans exert positive direction and effective screening of proposals, the program of the institution becomes segmented.

[14] See, for example, the writings of Mary Parker Follett, Chester I. Barnard, Elton Mayo, and Herbert A. Simon.

university can find common purposes sufficient to ensure organic unity.

Academic expansion achieved decentralized structure when the organizational sinews to control decentralized units did not exist. Universities have lacked the development which Philip Selznick describes as follows: [15]

> The need for centralization declines as the homogeneity of personnel increases. A unified outlook, binding all levels of administration, will permit decentralization without damage to policy. When top leadership cannot depend on adherence to its viewpoint, formal controls are required, if only to take measures that will increase homogeneity. On the other hand, when the premises of official policy are well understood and widely accepted, centralization is more readily dispensable. Hence, we shall expect that a relatively high degree of centralization will be required in the early stages of institutional development. Later, when homogeneity has been achieved, decentralization will be feasible without undue loss of control.

2. Autonomous departmental organization has grown as an organizational aspect of the increase in man's knowledge. Since Prof. George Ticknor proposed that Harvard be organized by departments early in the last century, American higher education has had a growth characterized not only by a tremendous increase in students, but also by a concomitant increase in academic subjects. These subjects have become highly specialized and complex as man's increasing grasp of his physical and cultural environment has taken amazing strides unheard of in previous centuries.

The result is that departments not only enjoy a large degree of administrative autonomy, but are highly specialized in subject. The specialists who comprise their staffs tend to be the only ones who have sufficient grasp of their content for intelligent decision making. Indeed, some departments include a number of specialists who are unable to communicate with one another! Central institutional

---

[15] *Leadership in Administration*, Row, Peterson & Company, Evanston, Ill., 1957, p. 113. The author of this quotation would doubtless agree that in the university homogeneity once attained must be preserved. The centrifugal forces within the university necessitate a persistent effort to maintain a unified outlook.

leadership faces a very effective barrier imposed by the inability of administrators to comprehend the work of individual departments sufficiently to impose policies and personnel.

3. As a result of institutional size and of this specialization, the initiative for a great deal of educational policy, for personnel appointments and evaluation, and for the budgeting of equipment and educational facilities has shifted to departments. The basis of the power of departments lies in this initiative—a situation confirmed in the ten institutions studied for this report and in the analysis by Edward A. Doyle of 33 liberal arts colleges.[16]

Initiative power relates closely to size of institution and consequent decentralization of administrative units. Thus, among the institutions surveyed, departments proved strongest at the larger universities (Stanford, Minnesota, Georgetown, and Virginia).[17]

FUNCTION OF THE CHAIRMEN

The position of the chairman as official head of these administrative units varies both among institutions and with personalities. Thus, chairmen at Goucher College institutionally refrain from "running" their departments. At George Washington University, the executive officers of each department are usually younger members of the group; they are not accorded the formal responsibilities normally associated with departmental heads. Essentially they serve as administrative secretaries, and the older individual professors assume a large degree of independence. The chairmanships at Wesleyan University rotate annually, with the result that departmental policies tend to be made collaboratively by all members. At the University of Minnesota and at Stanford tradition has established

---

[16] *The Status and Functions of the Departmental Chairman,* The Catholic University of America Press, Washington, D.C., 1953. This view of the power of the department is further confirmed by Arthur J. Klein (ed.), *Adventures in the Reconstruction of Education,* Ohio State University College of Education, 1941.

[17] George Washington University proves an exception to this in that departments have lacked sufficient formal cohesion and individual professors tend to dominate much educational policy formulation.

prestige in the rank of full professor, and these departmental members wield great influence. Many other examples might be cited, yet these serve to illustrate the great variations in the roles of departmental chairmen.

Despite these variations, chairmen do have, on the whole, a decisive influence on budgeting, staffing, planning, reporting (for the department to the next person in the scalar organization), and directing research. Doyle's study makes clear, for example, that 69 per cent of the departmental chairmen participated directly in budget formulation and in the selection, promotion, and retention of academic staff members.

Within this general situation, some chairmen act as autocrats, firmly holding the reins of what power the department has, while others either encourage wide participation within their units in policy formulation or make little effort to exercise administrative leadership. In general, departmental chairmen in professional schools and colleges exercise much less influence and authority than their counterparts in liberal arts colleges. Many smaller professional schools lack departments and become in fact large departments themselves, with the dean as chairman. In others, probably because of the relative recency with which they changed from departmental to college or school organization, the position of the chairmen remains relatively weak; that of the dean, strong and executive.

Four relationships, on the whole, determine the functioning of departmental chairmen.

Relations with Other Administrators

Chairmen are only part-time administrators; that is, they devote only a part of their time to problems of budget and faculty compensation, selection, and promotion; to student admissions; to class scheduling; and to similar nonteaching or research tasks. Nearly all chairmen teach for a major portion of their time and are expected to maintain their scholarly productivity. Doyle's study disclosed that chairmen spend a third of their time with instructional matters and another quarter with advisement and student relations. Also, few chairmen receive specific compensation for the discharge of the responsibilities they carry as heads of their departments; in short, they are given little financial incentive to devote their time to the responsibilities of the chairmanship.

The department head has been likened to the foreman in industry. The foreman's role, it is said, is made difficult, and his effectiveness is limited, because he is neither fish nor fowl—he represents neither the management nor the workers. But the department head remains predominantly a teacher and a representative of his teaching colleagues. Even while he is looked to by his dean and his president as their representative and their channel of communication to the faculty, he remains basically a teacher in function and in loyalty.

This anomalous situation suggests that profitable further study might be made of the manner in which departmental chairmen discharge their administrative responsibilities. To what degree is institutional leadership limited by the lack of commitment on the part of chairmen to the institution's administrative officers, i.e., the dean and the president? If a chairman's part-time service prevents his effective discharge of administrative tasks, would it be feasible to merge, at least for administrative purposes, two or more related departments? Or might it be desirable, in large departments in large universities, to provide the chairmen with an administrative officer—not a man trained in the particular discipline, but one who is experienced in administration—to handle all administrative tasks? [18]

Relations with Departmental Associates

Chairmen uniformly make the initial recommendations (usually to deans) for appointments, promotions, and tenure commitments. Also, they have substantial control over semester schedules and instructional and other departmental assignments. As a result, chairmen do hold a position which assures them substantial influence over their departmental colleagues.[19] Thus, they can take

[18] Vice Provost R. S. Halford of Columbia University, who also served as chairman of the Department of Chemistry, is reported to have advanced this suggestion.

[19] In his book, *The Academic Man*, Logan Wilson discusses the chairmen's orientation to their administrative role. He points out that the "longer more

considerable initiative in gaining cooperation for educational developments and innovations. They are able to establish the character of the department (to stress teaching as against research, for example), which either enhances or detracts from institutional policies fostered by deans and presidents.

Definite limitations on this authority exist, however, in some institutions. At Cornell University the influence of senior faculty members frequently relegates a chairman to the position of presiding officer in departmental councils. At Princeton, most department chairmen seldom venture decisions without the supporting vote of all tenure members of the faculty. All departmental members participate in decisions at Wesleyan University, and senior professors hold decisive influence in the liberal arts and science departments at the University of Minnesota. At George Washington University, the executive officers of departments hold no general authority over academic personnel; they preside at meetings and communicate departmental decisions. At smaller institutions, like Beloit, Denison, Goucher, or Knox, particularly in those instances where many departments include not more than three or four members, the senior member exercises a substantial measure of decision-making authority, especially with respect to courses to be offered and the selection and promotion of faculty members.

Because in general they can gain cooperation from academic staffs and because they do serve as the primary means of communication between faculty and administration, chairmen can effectively support or undermine institutional policy which, in most instances, they have had some part in formulating. This implies a choice for institutional administration. The position of chairmen can be strengthened relatively, and they can be involved more closely in institutional decision making—to make them effective spearheads for institutional policy—or effort can be directed toward eliminating the influence of departments as adminis-

nearly permanent the tenure of office, the more authority the head customarily assumes or is delegated." Oxford University Press, New York, 1942, pp. 88ff.

trative units. Commitment to this latter philosophy has taken place at a number of institutions (such as Wesleyan and Goucher) by the establishment of divisional organization. At many such institutions, including Goucher College, chairmen have maintained their identity and control, however.

Relations with Students

In 32 of 33 colleges studied by Doyle, chairmen play a larger role as advisers to students majoring in their departments than do other members of the department. Undoubtedly, this holds more generally true for undergraduate students, graduate students being assigned to individual professors. But, overwhelmingly, chairmen do have responsibility for the educational advisement of their major students. They spend a considerable part of their nonteaching time in this activity, working out student programs and approving a variety of exceptions to departmental and other educational requirements.

This further emphasizes that the chairman is a key administrative person on the operating level. It illustrates the importance of a homogeneity of understood, institution-wide policy if the departmental organization is to further institutional purposes effectively.

Relations with Faculty Governing Units

While chairmen exercise substantial authority over educational policy within their departments, they do not—in terms of their administrative positions—generally serve on committees and councils of the general faculty. In most institutions, departmental decisions on courses and curriculum face review, to a varying degree, by school or institution-wide faculty committees and councils. In some universities (the University of California, for example), all new courses must be approved by the faculty curriculum committee. In these institutions, the departments' power lies in their prerogative to initiate proposals.

This situation poses several problems. On the one hand, it makes difficult the development of educational programs crossing departmentally defined areas of knowledge. On the other hand, it limits the effectiveness of the chairman to whatever he can accomplish through persuasion of his departmental colleagues, and then through persuading the representatives of other departments serving on general faculty committees. This is a democratic and a slow process. Many men who are well trained, experienced, and accomplished in teaching and research lack the requisite skills for bringing about educational advance through the typical structure of a university.

BASIC PROBLEM: EFFECTING LEADERSHIP THROUGH DEPARTMENTAL STRUCTURE

As the basic unit of the administrative structure, departments have the power to initiate most actions that affect the basic function of the institution. They have the opportunity, and in some institutions almost exclusive authority, to propose changes in courses and curricula, to propose the selection or promotion of faculty members, and to suggest changes in conditions affecting the student in the classroom, e.g., absences. At the same time, they form the basic units which ultimately carry out, properly or inadequately, the policies of the institution. Because of this power of initiative and of ultimate implementation—in the sense of Chester Barnard that final authority lies with the person to whom it is addressed [20]—the desires of governing boards, presidents, and deans have effect to the degree that they can generate effective leadership.

In the departmental organization of most universities and colleges, the department chairman does hold substantial personal authority because of his influence over personnel policies and instructional assignments and his position in the formal communication between faculty members and administration.

[20] In the final analysis, Barnard proposes, authority depends upon acceptance by individuals or groups involved. They either accept or reject the instructions of an administrative superior. Thus, an order must be understood, believed, compatible to the recipient's net advantage of connection with the organization, and in line with the recipient's ability to carry it out.

The above suggests two considerations. First, the departmental structure can serve, and often does, as a bastion of the *status quo* in opposition to any creative educational leadership. David Riesman aptly likens the departments to political and social blocks and groupings in society: "Each prevents the others from growing too big, from encompassing too much." Each acts to prevent new potential disciplines from becoming established as competitors for funds and students.[21] On the other hand, the department structure can serve as the means by which presidents, provosts, and deans can make effective their leadership. It can serve in this capacity if departmental chairmen effectively participate with deans, provosts, and presidents in considering educational issues and in formulating institutional policies and programs, and then accept the responsibility for and are capable of leading their departmental colleagues in putting such policies and programs into effect.

Second, within the framework of these two possibilities, the chairmen are the key personnel for administrative relations with faculty members and with students. Therefore, the position and responsibilities, administratively, of chairmen offer a fruitful area for scrutiny. To the degree that chairmen primarily associate themselves with their colleagues, they will tend to reinforce the decentralized, autonomous nature of academic organization. Thus, they will tend, more often than not, to reinforce existing educational philosophies and commitments and resist educational change. To the degree that they recognize their administrative responsibilities, chairmen can better implement institutional policies and creatively participate in formulating policies.

This is not to suggest that all new ideas for educational advance will come "down from above." Surely the chairman's responsibility includes the presentation and promotion, with dean and others, of the ideas initiated by his departmental colleagues. Observation suggests that more often he is called upon to relay, to his departmental colleagues, ideas that have originated in other departments or with the dean, president, or others. In this role he is relied upon

[21] David Riesman, *Constraint and Variety in American Education*, University of Nebraska Press, Lincoln, Nebr., 1956, p. 94.

to perform an administrative responsibility that he often refuses to accept! The departmental chairman in the typical American university is a (if not *the*) key administrative officer. Hence, there is need for much more thoughtful analysis of what he does and what he might do than yet exists. Scholars who will focus their research on the manner of selection of chairmen (e.g., Can you get "good" chairmen by election? Will the faculty permit their appointment by dean or president?), on their tenure, on the qualifications of individuals who serve, on the functions the chairman is expected —and permitted—to perform, and on the techniques successful chairmen use, can make a large contribution.

The scholar of university governance who would essay this task should study the following provocative and impassioned statement included by Chancellor Kimpton in his 1959 annual report: [22]

. . . A great deal can be said, incidentally, for the old *head* of a department. . . . He was appointed for life, it was his department, and he ran it. The running of a department was a career, as important to the head as his own research and teaching, and sometimes far more so. All decisions were his after whatever consultation he chose to engage in; but he knew that the stature of his department was his own stature in the university and in the academic world in general. There were some great department heads in those days, and, more important, there were some great departments. I still share enough of the faculty resentment for the administrator to realize that the old system had to go, but there are some lessons here for us. What is everybody's responsibility is nobody's responsibility, and a present-day chairman must have more of a function than presiding at meetings. He must be selected with great care by the faculty and the administration, and he must be armed with real power. Of course, he should consult with his senior colleagues before any major moves, but he can become immobilized by too much democratic razzle-dazzle. Above all else, the department must be his real responsibility, rather than a rotating chore that he reluctantly assumes for his allotted term. The chairman of the department is the one the administration of the university can trust in the all-important business of promotions; and it is on him that the future quality of the university rests.

[22] *Op. cit.*, p. 10.

COMPLEXITY OF ACADEMIC OFFICERS' TASKS

One of the most significant observations to be made of the governance of American colleges and universities in the late 1950s has to do with the expanding role of the academic officers: the deans and department heads. Increasingly, responsibility for decision making in the central areas of educational governance is being entrusted, not by design but by the pressure of events, to the deans and the department heads. As institutions grow larger and the tasks of central administration, particularly the all-consuming task of financing, consume the time of the president, the prime areas of decision making—for educational programing and for faculty selection and promotion—are entrusted to deans and to department heads.

More precisely, it should be said that these responsibilities are entrusted first to deans and then, as their time is consumed by administration, to department heads. The president and progressively the dean tend to become withdrawn from the educational councils of the institution by the demands of administration. For effective decision making in the important educational areas, the deans, and even more the department heads, bear three substantial handicaps.

1. Each is "in between" the expectations of the administration on the one side and the faculty on the other. Much more than any counterpart in industrial or governmental organization the dean and the department head are looked to to represent their subordinates while being expected by their superiors to voice the views of the administration.

2. In representing the administration, it is these officers that face the substantial specialization of their faculties. The naïve assumption that prevails in many organizations that the supervisor "knows more" is nowhere less applicable than in the college faculty. The academic officer often must make decisions about educational program and the competence of individual teachers with little knowledge or appreciation of their specialties.

3. In representing the faculty, each department head (and in the university, the dean) voices the views of a narrow segment of the whole institution. Few are able to think comprehensively in terms of the needs and interests of *all* departments, and of *all* schools that constitute the aggregate of knowledge that is to be integrated in a program adapted to the needs of the oncoming generation.

These handicaps are analogous to those suffered by "middle management" in other kinds of organizations. Yet the relationships between the deans, and especially the department heads, and the faculty are such that these handicaps are substantially greater for those who are looked to to perform the middle management role in the college or university.

Finally, the statement of these handicaps is premised on an assumption that is generally accepted for industrial, governmental, and military organizations, but often questioned in the college or university. This assumption is that the needs and goals of the whole organization are primary. Many serving on today's faculties question the assumption that what is good for the department of English is good for the college of arts and sciences, the university, the students, and the supporting society!

Chapter 5

THE ROLE OF FACULTIES IN GOVERNANCE

A PRIMARY DIFFERENCE between the college or university and other forms of enterprise, so far as administration is concerned, lies in the authority and responsibility placed in the faculty, as a body, by tradition,[1] by custom, or by formal bylaw or regulation. A second difference lies in the freedom of speech and of thought accorded the faculty member as an individual. Together these two factors have organizational and administrative consequences that are unparalleled in business or governmental enterprise. Together they suggest that if more is to be learned about how colleges and universities are governed effectively, it is essential that intensive, unemotional analysis be given to the question: What role do faculties play, and what responsibilities should they have in the governance of colleges and universities?

The beginnings of faculty participation in governance in American colleges and universities, unfortunately, have never been

[1] Benjamin Rush, an early trustee of Dickinson College (Pennsylvania) is reported to have written in a letter to his fellow trustees, Oct. 21, 1876, "When our professors cease to be qualified to share in the power of the College, it will be proper to dismiss them, for government and instruction are inseparably connected." Quoted in Richard O. Hofstadter and Walter P. Metzger, *The Development of Academic Freedom in the United States,* Columbia University Press, New York, 1955, pp. 218ff.

traced with care and thoroughness. Yet evidences of the faculty's role are available. It is known, for example, that since the early eighteenth century, the faculty at Harvard has formed what has been described as the "immediate government"; since the early 1800s the faculty has constituted a body authorized to exercise substantial powers granted it by the corporation. At Yale, starting with the presidency of Jeremiah Day (1817–1846), strong precedents were established that all questions connected with educational policy would be decided in a meeting of the faculty, and that no faculty member would be appointed without the consent of the faculty of which he was to become a member. Similarly, Thomas Jefferson, when he established the University of Virginia (opened in 1825), stipulated that members of the faculty would have substantial freedom in determining courses of study and maintaining discipline, and as a group broad authority to make decisions about educational program and membership on the faculty. These and other precedents set a tradition that has influenced the governance of American colleges and universities since those early days.[2]

THE ENIGMA OF FACULTY DECISION MAKING

The inheritors of this tradition, today's faculty members, generally manifest a catholic concern and a claim to comprehensive competence in a wide assortment of matters of institutional policy and administration. The breadth of their claim is illustrated by the report of the Special Committee on Faculty Organization and Procedures at Cornell University (April, 1957). This report on "the functions of the University Faculty" claims responsibility for the faculty for "initiating, considering, and making recommendations on questions of educational policy or problems arising therefrom, whether concerning (i) current operations of the University, or (ii) long-range policy (such as admission policies, proposals for new degrees, establishment of new educational and research units, the size of the University, auxiliary cultural agencies, and

[2] See Hofstadter and Metzger, op. cit., pp. 234–238, for discussion of faculty participation in governing decisions in the "old-time college."

questions concerning the status and privileges of the Faculty)." And the report interprets the term "questions of educational policy" broadly to include questions that involve "(i) conditions facilitating instruction, study research, publication and other scholarly activities of faculty members and students or (ii) the general welfare of the academic community."

The faculty's right to be consulted and to make decisions on educational questions is generally claimed [3] and usually acknowledged. Yet their influence in governance is repeatedly challenged as institutions grow larger and the demands of administration create central staffs about the president and the deans which tend to accumulate authority for decision making. The faculty's influence is further reduced by an apparent indifference and unwillingness (of many faculty members) to devote time to consideration of those questions on which the faculty's advice or decision is sought.[4]

These enigmatic attitudes of faculties—a catholic concern and a comprehensive claim of competence, on the one hand, and an indifference and unwillingness to take part, on the other, give rise to several questions on the part faculties can and should play in institutional decision making.

What is the preferable distribution of responsibilities for governance? In other words, what decisions should be made by the trustees? By the president? By the deans? By the general faculty? By the faculties of schools or departments?

What kinds of decisions do faculties have special competence to

[3] "It ought to be, and commonly is agreed that in all matters of educational policy the responsible action of the faculty should not be abrogated except in dire necessity. To overrule such action is, in effect, to censure the faculty and to imply that the machinery of academic government has broken down." Max Black, F. G. Marcham, and George Winter, "Faculty-Trustee Relations," *AAUP Bulletin*, 42:613–624, 1956, p. 615.

[4] "Every faculty member believes it is his right to participate in decisions of importance to higher education, yet few understand the nature of higher education outside their own departmental activities." An opinion included in the summary of a discussion by the trustees of the Carnegie Foundation for the Advancement of Teaching entitled *The Education of College Teachers*, The Foundation, 1958, p. 15.

make? For what kinds of decisions do they have little or no capability? What characteristics or attitudes limit their effectiveness in contributing to educational decisions?

How adequate are the organizational mechanisms through which faculties customarily voice their views?

ORGANIZATIONAL MECHANISMS

The organizational machinery through which the individuals who serve on college and university faculties are enabled to participate in institutional governance must be viewed at three levels. Departments, made up of all teachers and scholars in a subject-matter field or discipline, exist in every institution studied. Schools, or colleges, have their separate faculties and their separate faculty organizations in each university. And in each university there are mechanisms through which the several faculties (of departments and of schools throughout the institution) function as a university-wide faculty and consider matters affecting more than one school or college.

The departmental faculty seldom becomes an important organizational mechanism until the faculty attains a membership of 100 or more. For example, in Goucher College with a faculty of 76, including both full-time and part-time members, some individual departments have 3 or fewer members. In a university, on the other hand, departmental faculties will have 30 to 50 or more members. There the departmental faculty may be the major vehicle for faculty involvement. In these institutions, the departmental faculty will likely have regular meetings, a secretary in addition to a chairman, and bylaws specifying its organization and processes.

The school faculty is the principal mechanism for faculty involvement in governance in the independent college. There, where the full-time faculty is relatively small, i.e., from 75 at Grinnell to 100 at Wesleyan and 101 at Carleton, the total membership meets as a body and often engages vigorously in debate. It may also function through a number of committees, sometimes entirely too many (20 or more) to conserve teachers' time. The larger school faculties, like the School of Humanities and Sciences at

Stanford, will have an "executive committee or council" made up of the dean, assistant deans, and department heads. Many school faculties have their organization and processes formally established in published bylaws.

The school faculty is the usual form of organization in all professional schools, save the largest. There the group is small enough to meet as a body, and specialized subject-matter lines are not so rigidly drawn as among the members of a college of arts and sciences. The school or college faculty, as it becomes larger, will likely be organized into a number of committees. In some institutions only the tenure members of the faculty will be privileged to participate in the school faculty, or a separate "academic council" made up only of the president and full professors (e.g., as at Wesleyan University) exercises authority over matters of major consequence.

The university-wide faculty becomes so large (e.g., University of Virginia, 430 full-time; Stanford University, 567 full-time; and the University of Minnesota, with a faculty of more than 3,000) in the major universities that it can function only through some representative body. At the University of Washington, for example, both a senate and a general faculty organization exist.[5] The voting membership of the university faculty consists of the president, the vice president, and all full-time teaching personnel. The university senate, a small body elected from the voting membership of the faculty, is the legislative and executive agency of the university faculty. The faculty has enacted regulations for the government of the university and for sharing responsibility with the president and academic deans in well-defined matters. More than twenty-five faculty committees exist with specified duties and powers.[6] The senate, through its executive committee, advises the president on general educational policies.

The organizational mechanisms that are used to enable faculties

[5] This description of the organization of the University of Washington faculty is based on James D. Thompson, *Report on Organizational Relationships in Certain Universities*, a report prepared for the faculty of the University of Pittsburgh, March, 1958.

[6] Goucher College, with a faculty of only 76, had 24 committees in 1958.

to participate in governance vary markedly. Even where the same form, e.g., a senate, exists in two institutions, its authority and function will vary substantially. Yet in most institutions mechanisms exist, and those that have been pictured are illustrative of their form. Far more important than their form is the substance with which they deal and the authority they exercise.

IN EDUCATIONAL POLICIES

Practice concerning faculty participation varies. At institutions such as Denison and Wesleyan, faculties effect an informal but decisive influence. At larger institutions, such as the University of Virginia and Cornell University, tradition has given faculties formally a very strong hand, against which presidents press with relative ineffectiveness. At the other extreme, presidents at Jesuit universities, such as Georgetown, have a strong influence via their fellow members of the religious order who serve as deans, rectors, and chairmen and who control policies. At the University of Minnesota the president can set aside decisions of the institution-wide university senate. But the effective power to initiate significant educational actions lies with the faculties of many departments, schools, and institutes, and the president holds only a veto power. At smaller institutions, such as the University of Toledo, the president will afford the faculty an opportunity to voice its views, but retains for himself and the governing board the unqualified right of decision.

These illustrations indicate that the authority of faculties to make decisions about educational practices and programs varies among institutions. By and large, however, the faculty [7] usually

[7] The breadth of faculty concern is illustrated by two reports of subunits of the American Association of University Professors. "The Place and Function of Faculties in College and University Government" (a report of "Committee T" of the AAUP, 1955) included, among other items, an analysis of the extent to which the faculties of more than 300 institutions were consulted "in choice of new president," "in selection of deans," "in making budget," etc. The *Report of the Committee on Faculty Administration Relationships* of the University of Minnesota Chapter of the AAUP (May, 1957) canvasses the extent to which

claims authority to decide questions of curriculum, degrees, examinations, entrance requirements, academic standards, and related questions without formal approval or even consideration by the president or governing board. With respect to educational issues having substantial financial implications, the faculty will be authorized to (or often will insist upon the right to) express its judgment, even though the president and governing board reserve the authority for final decision. If, for example, a college that served only a single sex were to consider the feasibility of becoming coeducational, if the total enrollment were to be materially increased, or if a traditionally liberal arts college were to add graduate work in teacher training, the faculties of most institutions would insist upon voicing an opinion which usually would materially influence the recommendation of the president and the final decision of the governing board.[8]

The relatively substantial authority that the faculty exercises over educational decisions in many institutions is founded more on tradition than on its formal establishment in university bylaws. For example, Dennison, in a study of eight liberal arts colleges, found that "in five of the eight colleges, the authority and responsibility of the faculty are referred to in codified legislation of the governing boards, but in only one, Vassar, is the delegation of authority sufficiently unrestricted to assure the faculty a free hand in matters assigned to it."[9] In two of the five institutions such authority as is granted to the faculty is explicitly subject to presidential approval.

One of the deadliest hazards to higher education is the resistance of faculties to change in subject matter and in method. This tendency is illustrated, in the institutions studied, by the disapproval of proposals (from fellow faculty members, a dean, or a president)

members of the faculties of the several schools of that university are consulted on educational and faculty membership questions.

[8] See discussion of this division of responsibility by B. K. Trippet, in an article entitled "The Role of a Faculty in College Administration," *AAUP Bulletin,* 43(3):484–491, September, 1957.

[9] Charles P. Dennison, *Faculty Rights and Obligations,* Teachers College, Columbia University, New York, 1955, p. 54.

for the establishment of new or the alteration of existing courses, the introduction of an interdisciplinary seminar for first- and second-year students, the changing of the basis for evaluating applications for admissions, the changing of teaching methods, and frequently, the placing of greater emphasis on general education.

Four factors significantly limit the capacity of the faculty as a body [10] to make efficient and progressive educational decisions:

1. Only a few institutions accumulate and have regularly available analytical data about the capacity of applicants for admission and about class size, course proliferation, and faculty work load to facilitate decision making.[11]

2. A minority among the members of most faculties have thought deeply and analytically about educational programs (e.g., curricula make-up), or teaching methods (e.g., size of class), or factors influencing instructional costs (e.g., course proliferation and size of class). Most faculty members are subject-matter specialists; few are educators in a comprehensive sense.

3. Much educational policy is formulated in bits and pieces, by the approval of a new course, the modification of a requirement for completion of a curriculum, or the alteration of an admission requirement. These bits and pieces seldom force comprehensive consideration of the educational program or prevailing practice.

4. Being subject-matter specialists, faculty members tend to resist proposals that, in their opinion, might encroach on the established preserves (e.g., number of courses offered, courses "required") of each subject-matter discipline.

The tendency of faculties to resist change usually means that the impetus for innovation—the establishment of new educational programs, new schools or colleges, new kinds of educational activities, e.g., a "junior year abroad"—comes from a dean or the president.[11] But it is only the persuasive, the tactful and forward-looking pres-

[10] This phrase *the faculty as a body* refers to the *general faculty*, i.e., the consolidated faculty of the whole institution, or to the faculty of a school within the institution, or to the faculty of a department.

[11] An illustration of such successful innovation by a president, J. E. W. Sterling of Stanford, is described in Robert Hoopes and Hubert Marshall, *The Undergraduate in the University*, Stanford University Press, 1957, pp. v–vii, 1–2, and

ident or dean, with educational goals clearly in mind, who brings about academic progress over the tendency of the faculty to resist change and over their usual right of veto. Unfortunately, a small portion of all presidents and deans have these requisite capacities. Fortunately, there are imaginative, progressive teachers on some faculties with the fortitude and the ability to lead their colleagues in effecting change in established educational programs and processes.

The influence of the administration in the decisions that constitute educational advance is usually exerted subtly through (1) the service by major officers, i.e., presidents and deans, as chairmen of faculty governing bodies; (2) the membership on faculties of these same administrative officers; (3) the appointment to faculty committees or as committee chairmen of individuals the presidents and/or deans know to be sympathetic with their ideas, or capable of generating educational forward movement; and (4) in a few instances, trustee-faculty consultation.

The central question is: Should the faculty's traditional right to decide educational issues be so comprehensive "that every matter involving educational policy is to be decided only by and with the consent of the faculty"? [12]

Observation of the governance of colleges and universities suggests that the answer should be no. The necessity for the continuing adaptation of educational program to society's changing needs, and the tendency of faculties, unobserving of the evolving demands of society or addicted to the practice of "departmental courtesy," to fight off changes in educational content or process, substantially disqualify most faculties for a large role in governance. Neither the assurance of academic freedom nor the faculty's superior understanding of what should be taught, and how, makes it essential

---

84. A second illustration is the effort of Chancellor Edward H. Litchfield at the University of Pittsburgh to modify the academic calendar and to focus the university's educational program on the provision of "*both* a liberal education and a professional training."

[12] Trippet, *op. cit.*, p. 488.

that the faculty should have the exclusive right to determine what education shall be offered.

What is needed is not, as Ruml has contended, that "the Trustees [or the president one might add] . . . must take back from the faculty as a body its present authority over the design and administration of the curriculum." [13] What is needed is greater collaboration than obtains in most institutions among trustees and president, deans and faculty, in continually evaluating and reshaping the educational program. The interest and the capacity of the ablest trustees and presidents are ineffectively utilized if they are limited to the exercise of judgment on administrative and financial matters.

IN FACULTY PERSONNEL POLICIES

Faculty members—humanly and naturally—take an active interest in decisions on personnel issues. They expect to be consulted—and usually are—on tenure policies, merit plans, sabbatical leave arrangements, retirement provisions, and various fringe benefits.

Individual faculty members usually participate in handling appointments, promotions, and tenure commitments as members of their departmental or school faculty. The effective power to appoint and to promote, in most universities, rests with the subject-matter departments and their chairmen.[14] The deans review and forward to presidents, who approve and forward to trustees for their "rubber stamping." In this central aspect of faculty personnel administration the "department chairmen are key figures." [15] Indeed the chairmen play the primary role in the recruitment of new faculty members.[16]

Variations in practice are common. In some institutions the de-

[13] Beardsley Ruml and Donald H. Morrison, *Memo to a College Trustee,* McGraw-Hill Book Company, Inc., New York, 1959, p. 13.

[14] One department chairman explained to the author that he had on two occasions explained to his dean, more recently come to the institution, that the general faculty would not approve the appointment of a new faculty member if it originated with the dean rather than in a departmental faculty!

[15] See Theodore Caplow and Reece J. McGee, *The Academic Marketplace,* Basic Books, Inc., New York, 1958, p. 186.

[16] *Ibid.*

partmental chairman serves as "chairman" and presides when decisions on new appointees and on tenure promotions are made by all tenure members of the faculty as a body. In these situations the full professors and older members of departments often have large influence in the making of decisions.

Limitations upon the chairmen's authority, usually to protect the influence of departmental members, are found in a number of institutions.

At most institutions, faculties do voice recommendations on policies, even if not on individual selections, promotions, and salary increases. At Princeton a department head seldom acts without obtaining the approval of his colleagues. At George Washington University, the members of some departments interview applicants and have an opportunity to vote on the desirability of a candidate. At several institutions faculty bodies or committees have an opportunity to review appointments and promotions with the presidents. At Denison University, for example, an elected advisory committee meets with the president. The University of Minnesota has a faculty consultative committee that discusses with the president policies governing faculty selection, promotion, and compensation. At Stanford University, new appointments are considered carefully by the provost in behalf of the president and are submitted by the president to a faculty advisory board. Georgetown University has a salary, rank, and tenure committee which reviews most appointments to the instructional staff before the president acts.

On questions of salary increase, the locus of decision making shifts to the department head and to the dean or president. The department head is asked to recommend from among his colleagues those who should receive salary increases. These recommendations are submitted to the dean or to the president. The authority to decide rests effectively with the president in most institutions, and with the dean in the larger institutions.

In summary, it appears clear that at most institutions the whole faculty does *not* often vote on appointments. At a minority of all universities, e.g., Princeton and Stanford, a senior committee representing the university faculty will review all proposed appointments and promotions to tenure positions with the president or his aides. In few, if any, instances does the faculty pass upon individual salary increases.[17]

FINANCIAL AFFAIRS AND CAPITAL IMPROVEMENTS

The role of the faculty in making financial decisions in most colleges and universities is small in theory and large in fact. Few institutions provide for faculty participation in the determination of the annual budget, other than as each department is permitted to recommend its annual financial needs. A notable exception is the University of Minnesota, where a faculty committee reviews the annual budget with the president prior to his recommendations to the state legislature.

Yet at a number of institutions the faculties protest from time to time the provision made in the annual budget for administrative services and staffs, athletics, and special projects of a noneducational nature. More significantly, in many institutions the faculty, in pressing for expansion of the faculty and increases in faculty salaries, exercises a considerable influence over the annual budget for instructional salaries and incidental expenses which normally constitute almost half of the total budget.[18]

The degree to which faculties have a voice in the construction of new buildings or additions to physical plant depends upon the attitude of a particular administration and primarily of the president. Physical plant decisions, e.g., the determination of what buildings shall be built, rest uniformly with presidents and governing boards. Yet, the president who, as at the University of Virginia, approves the construction of a student union before a needed educational facility is provided for will face—and cannot overlook—faculty criticism which may well affect his relations on other matters.

Faculties frequently contend that they should advise on the rela-

[17] An exception to this generalization, it is said, exists in the University of California. There the faculty exercises a greater influence over individual salaries.
[18] See *A Study of Income and Expenditures in Sixty Colleges, Year 1953–54*, National Federation of College and University Business Officers Associations, 1955.

tive need for dormitories, gymnasiums, athletic fields, laboratories, or classrooms, and with respect to the two latter types of buildings, on the form they must take to facilitate their educational use. At the University of Akron about ten years ago, faculty members bitterly protested a decision to improve physical plant before raising faculty salaries. Similarly, at the University of Virginia the faculty (and students also) made known their preference for laboratory and classroom buildings over a student union. At Stanford a faculty committee has long had a meaningful part in making plans for the development of that institution's land resources, both those developed as an industrial, income-producing area, and those acres utilized as campus and as the faculty residential area.

In long-range perspective, the practice of consulting the faculty or a faculty committee (even on the subject of faculty salaries) has proven a sound one. This practice tends to establish among the central staff of the educational enterprise a cohesiveness and sense of responsibility for decisions. To deny the faculty's capacity intelligently to participate or their interest in financial matters and capital improvements can prove detrimental. These areas of decision relate too closely to educational matters.

As in other enterprises—business, religious, scientific—it is apparent that as the intellectual level of the staff rises, the more insistent is the demand of the staff to be consulted and the more comprehensive the range of issues on which consultation is expected. Against the advantages of involving faculty members in collaborative effort—and it is clear that the process of consultation strengthens their allegiance to the institution and their individual zeal and satisfaction—stand some reservations. Do faculties have time for participation in decision making on issues of physical development and finance? Do faculty members have a sufficiently broad understanding of the total operation to participate intelligently in making such decisions? How and to what degree can such views and time as they have be incorporated in the decision-making process? These and similar questions which relate to the increasing size and complexity of modern higher institutions need to be given careful consideration.

IN STUDENT AFFAIRS

Decisions relative to student admissions, discipline, recreation, government, and related matters—fields traditionally subject to faculty control—have been more and more turned over in recent years to administrative supervision.[19] Deans of students and their staffs, armed with an increasingly extensive knowledge of psychological tests and sociological insights, have taken over the direction of student affairs. These academic officers serve as presidential aides rather than faculty representatives. Faculty committees on admissions do exist in many institutions—usually having more influence in the smaller colleges—but serve primarily in conjunction with student deans. As in other aspects of academic administration, size and complexity of the problem have combined with an increasingly intellectual and specialized orientation of faculty members to effect this shift to administrative direction.[20]

Similarly, the emergence of the dean of students—a new field of specialized competence—has tended to reduce the responsibility of the faculty for decision making relative to discipline (when action outside the classroom merits punishment), recreation (when dances or other functions may be held and under what conditions), and government (who shall control student publications). The dean of students will usually work under the guidance of a faculty committee, but he is usually directly responsible to a dean, a provost, an academic vice president, or the president. The companion tides of increasing specialization and growing enrollments have run against faculty handling of this function.

In the smaller colleges—illustrated by Beloit, Carleton, Denison, Goucher, and others—a low student-faculty ratio permits faculty

[19] In his biography of Hopkins, F. Rudolph has given an excellent account of the orientation of the early American colleges to the personal and moral life of students and their discipline. *Mark Hopkins and the Log,* Yale University Press, New Haven, Conn., 1956.

[20] Thus, at the University of Toledo a faculty-student activities committee ten years ago became an administrative body with three student personnel officers and two faculty members. At Stanford University, the committee on student affairs is classified as "administrative" and appointed by the president.

members to maintain more intimate student relations. There the faculty exercises a greater voice in student affairs.

At a number of institutions, notably the University of Virginia and Wesleyan University, student honor systems, traditionally supervised and controlled by students, exercise a larger than usual influence over decisions relative to discipline, recreation, and even academic discipline. Despite those individual cases, as universities grow large, the deciding of questions on student affairs tends to become institutionalized and to be performed by a dean (or deans) of students, with the advice of a faculty committee.

The emergence of the dean of students gives rise to differences of opinion between the practitioners of this new occupational specialty and faculties. The faculty may think students' shelter needs are met by plain, inexpensive dormitories; the dean of students may press for more expensive, comfortable living quarters. The faculty may expect the dean of students to mete out punishment with a firm hand, while he may conclude that infractions of rules, e.g., absence before a holiday, merit only a warning. The dean of students' counsel to students to aid them in adjusting to campus life may be regarded by the faculty as meaningless or conflicting with the counsel the student should obtain from his instructor. These differences may be ameliorated by regular consultation between the dean of students and an advisory faculty committee, but the differences are rooted in different values and tend to arise on many campuses.[21]

IN PUBLIC AND ALUMNI RELATIONS

The faculty has a considerable effect upon, and in turn is considerably affected by, public and alumni attitudes. But in the determination of policies and programs relating to public and alumni

[21] T. R. McConnell, University of California (Berkeley), effectively describes and analyzes the causes and significances of these differences in "The Relation of Institutional Goals and Organization of the Administration of Student Personnel Work," in Martin L. Snoke (ed.), Approaches to the Study of Administration in Student Personnel Work, Minnesota Studies in Student Personnel Work, no. 9, University of Minnesota Press, Minneapolis, 1960, pp. 19–35.

relations, and to fund raising, the faculty as such (with the possible exception of a few individual members) rarely plays an appreciable role.

What formal consideration faculty groups give to these matters usually results from outside pressures directed against the academic operation or against individual faculty members. Thus, in recent years faculty bodies took serious cognizance in most institutions of attacks against so-called radicalism or communism among teachers. Some of the policies related to employment security result from such public relations incidents. Conversely, such policies tend to reinforce the isolation of faculties from publics to which universities and colleges must look for support. Such policies add difficulty to administrators' task of coordinating the activities within their institutions with outside groups.

As individuals, a small minority of all faculty members are able to help, or are interested in helping, with alumni or public relations or with fund raising. The orientation of faculty members, in relations outside their institutions, is to their professional associates. When a professor turns to outside activities, he tends to do so in terms of his subject-matter discipline. He speaks as an authority on some phase of knowledge. He writes articles for professional journals and attends professional meetings. He thinks in terms of law, of medicine, of economics; as an engineer; or as an eduactor.

The importance of public and alumni relations to ends which the faculties deem important, e.g., the raising of admission standards, the financing of a new library, or the raising of faculty salaries, argues strongly for involving the faculty in public and alumni affairs. At the least their advice is required in explaining the reasoning on which new admission standards are founded (especially as they affect alumni children!) or the need for a new library. Their involvement also serves to broaden the academics' sensitivities to matters beyond departmental concern and to enlarge their identification with the whole institution. A minority of all faculty members will believe they have time, after meeting their teaching and research schedules, to contribute to public and alumni relations. Few may be effective in framing policies or programs to mobilize public or alumni support, or in influencing the opinions of these groups. But the faculty's dependence (not always recognized) on these groups, to achieve dearly sought ends, indicates the obligation of its members to participate when and as they are able.

A SUMMARY OF FACULTY ROLE

The central objective of a college or university is the translation of the talents and capacities of its faculty into significant educational results. Most major policy or program decisions, hence, have relevance to this central objective. With these decisions the faculty may be expected to manifest a concern. To the making of many decisions the faculty as a body, or individual faculty members, are capable of important contributions.

Is the role of the faculty in the governance of American colleges and universities consistent with their concern and their capabilities? The following summary of observations on the part faculties play provides an answer to this important question.[22]

1. Faculty influence on institutional governance is greatest in the realm of educational policy. Their effectiveness in contributing to such decisions is limited by the lack of analytical data on which to base objective and considered decisions, the limited interest of many faculty members in higher education, their tendency to think about and act upon specific courses or requirements rather than policies, and their primary concern with their individual subject-matter fields.

Despite these limitations upon their effectiveness, faculties tend to claim large and sometimes exclusive authority over educational

[22] These observations are supported (at least in substantial part) by a report prepared by James D. Thompson of the University of Pittsburgh. His *Report on Organizational Relationships in Certain Universities*, Mar. 7, 1958, prepared for the Committee on Faculty Participation in Policy Making at the University of Pittsburgh, deals with "arrangements for faculty participation in university policy, as found in sixteen American universities." These universities are California, Chicago, Columbia, Harvard, Indiana, Michigan, Minnesota, New York, Northwestern, Princeton, Stanford, Tulane, Vanderbilt, Washington, Wesleyan (Conn.), and Yale.

decisions. In addition, some faculty members and some faculties see educational implications in most decisions the institution makes. Hence, they assert an authority which abridges the responsibilities of the institution's officers and trustees for fiscal, legal, public relations, and other noneducational decisions.

2. The attitudes of trustees, and especially presidents, toward faculty participation in decisions on other than narrowly defined "educational" questions vary from institution to institution, and within institutions from one regime to the next. In a few institutions widespread participation is sought; in others some participation is tolerated, not sought; while in others what is sought is not the faculty's views but its approval of proposals of administrators. In some institutions, trustees and administrative officials obviously would like to give the faculty a greater sense of participation without being embarrassed by the results. There are few recorded instances where faculties have organized as protective or pressure groups (usually in chapters of the American Association of University Professors) in which they have improved significantly their individual benefits or exercised substantial influence on the institution's policies.

3. The organizational arrangements through which faculty members are enabled to voice their views on university-wide policy questions are seldom able to bring about the participation of most members. The result, especially in the larger institutions, is a widening gap in understanding between the university officers and trustees and the "working faculty."

4. The proportion of the total faculty that participates through these organizational arrangements in decision making is further limited by (a) the limitation of voting rights to "tenure faculty members" or to those with the rank of assistant professor and above, (b) the denial of voting rights to relatively large numbers of part-time faculty members, and (c) the failure of many faculty members to attend university-wide faculty or senate meetings when faculty discussion or approval is required.

These conclusions suggest the extent of faculty participation in decision making. They do not explain the administration-faculty friction that obtains in many institutions. Faculty representatives resent what they call highhanded administrative action in areas of their primary concern. Administrative officers seek more efficient and effective practices in times when income fails to grow with expenses, and they press for innovations. They frequently feel that their efforts to bring about progress are hindered or blocked by faculty prerogatives.

Underlying this friction is the basic fact that faculty members adhere to a cause "greater than" their institutions.[23] They have a professional allegiance to knowledge and intellectual freedom which supersedes their institutional loyalties. Administrators are more organization-oriented. The result is an organizational weakness: a lack of institution-wide sense of destiny or purpose which guides decision making and coordinates participants.

Still other causes of this friction are apparent:

1. Differing concerns with higher education. The president, and sometimes the dean, is concerned with the idea and the ideals of higher education, or at least with the function of the whole institution; most faculty members are primarily concerned with their own work and disciplines, and only secondarily, if at all, with higher education.

2. The "in-between" position of the president and the dean. The president is between the faculty and the trustees, the alumni, or the legislature. The dean is between his faculty and the president, and, in the larger institutions, the president's staff, i.e., the provost, academic vice president, comptroller, and others. The faculty, hence, is often not "sure" of the reflection of their views to those who will, in the end, make the decision.

3. Complexity of purpose. The multiplicity and diversity of purposes of the expanding university inevitably mean that the general faculty includes individuals and subgroups striving to

---

[23] Paul F. Lazarsfeld and Wagner Thielens, Jr., have testified to this faculty point of view. They found, for example, that 65 per cent of the faculty members whose views they assembled placed the rights of scholars above the reputation of their institution in matters involving academic freedom. *The Academic Mind*, Free Press, Glencoe, Ill., 1958, p. 141.

serve different and sometime conflicting purposes. It means that the president, concerned with the whole institution, is confronted with many difficulties in reconciling diverse views.

4. Increasing size. The growth of many universities tends to remove the president from direct contact with faculty members and faculty governing units. Delegation of presidential responsibility has given many faculty groups an unsatisfying relationship with the administration and a feeling that their desires are not communicated properly to presidents, or to governing boards.

5. Poor communications. At few colleges and universities do we find evidence of conscious effort to develop effective communications. In part this reflects the political overtones of "getting things done" by quiet maneuvering among participants at the cost of open explanations and clearly enunciated plans and policies.

6. Lack of operational and administrative research that would provide the factual data which would make for more objective, as well as more thorough, consideration.[24]

PROBLEMS REQUIRING FURTHER STUDY

This survey of the role of faculties in governance reveals questions for which answers must be found. Those scholars of administration or educational administrators who would make our colleges and universities adequate to their expanding job must distill from the experience of existing institutions answers to such questions as these:

Should university-wide faculties or school faculties be delegated final authority to decide matters of educational policy? Or should they serve as advisers to presidents and deans?

What role should the president play in relation to the faculty? Should he serve as chairman of the faculty, presiding at meetings of the senate and key committees and actively participating as the

[24] For further consideration of causes of administration-faculty friction see R. M. Sullivan, "Administrative-Faculty Relationships in Colleges and Universities," *Journal of Higher Education*, 27:308–326, 349, June, 1956. This article presents the results of a study of relationships in eighteen colleges and universities, sponsored by the Carnegie Corporation.

senior among equals in faculty debates? Or should he hold himself apart as (1) the institution's chief executive, to whom faculty recommendations go for approval, or (2) the head of a separate but parallel branch of the institution's government?

How much and what kind of communication should exist between faculty governing bodies and trustees, and how frequently? What responsibility should the president accept for seeing to it that the communication between faculty and trustees is fully adequate to the needs of each?

How can faculties be helped to consider the institution's policy problems in terms of the whole institution and as problems of higher education, rather than in terms of the interests of scholars in a single discipline? And how can a major proportion of all faculty members be interested in those problems on which their views should be had? What arrangements best serve to ensure considered attention by the faculty and reflection of a representative faculty viewpoint without claiming unduly of faculty members' time?

What organizational arrangements of departmental faculties, school faculties, university-wide senate, legislative council, or committees best serve to assemble faculty opinion for the benefit of officers and trustees? When should the president appoint committees, and when should committees be elected by the faculty?

Does the experience of the larger universities indicate that growth in the size of the institution and its faculty necessarily means that a university changes from a collective body of teachers and scholars to an employer-employee hierarchy?

Each of these questions must be studied in terms of the dynamics of institutional operations. What is needed is not formulas nor organization charts, but case studies that depict how presidents, deans, and faculties work, or do not work, together. What are needed are subtle analyses of how and why one president can persuade and lead a faculty toward educational progress, while in another institution a few professors can and do lead a faculty either to support a president who cannot prevail alone, or to further educational innovation that the president is not capable of leading—or opposes.

Chapter 6

THE UNIVERSITY: A CONTRAST
IN ADMINISTRATIVE PROCESS

THE ADMINISTRATION of any enterprise involves the making and subsequently the execution of a succession of decisions. In a manufacturing concern, these decisions involve the hiring of workers, the purchasing of raw materials, the determination of methods of production and volume of output, the setting of prices, and a myriad of related decisions of greater and lesser significance to the accomplishments of the enterprise. In a government bureau these decisions involve the proposal of legislation, the hiring and promotion of civil servants, the contracting with industry, the adjudication of cases, the formulation of budgets and work programs, and the determination of what shall be said to the public in speeches and reports.

In a university similar decisions are made and executed. Faculty members, administrators, coaches, secretaries, and various other persons are hired and promoted—or not promoted. A curriculum is formulated and reformulated; courses are added and dropped. Students are admitted or rejected, and once admitted they pose a series of disciplinary problems that require decisions. Tuition rates and fees are set. Budgets are made. Campaigns are launched for new funds; buildings are planned and constructed.

The effectiveness of any enterprise is related to the manner in

118

which such decisions are made, carried out, and remade. If such decisions are made effectively, they link together in a progressive and dynamic effort the participants within the enterprise and those without who supply essential resources (materials or finances) or who consume the product or services. In the manufacturing enterprise a succession of decisions must link together owners, managers, employees, bankers, suppliers, and customers in an expanding and mutually satisfying effort. In the university the continuum of decisions must relate the roles of trustees, administrators, faculty, staff, students, parents, alumni, donors, and, in public institutions, state legislators. The degree to which universities and colleges achieve this common effort demonstrates the effectiveness of the administrative organization.

THE UNIVERSALITY OF ADMINISTRATIVE PROCESS

Does the administrative process by which a university arrives at and carries out its decisions differ from that of a business firm or a governmental agency? Is the influence of board members less great or greater in the university than in the corporation? Must university executives—presidents and deans—possess skills not needed to the same degree by their counterparts in private and public business? And the faculty—does it play a greater, lesser, or different role than the core staff members of a business or a bureau?

The answers to these and related questions are not readily available in what has been written about the administration of colleges and universities. Yet the answers are needed. They are needed to help trustees, presidents, and faculties better understand their own institutions. They are needed to discourage loose generalizations about "administrative efficiency" founded on comparisons with business enterprise and governmental operations. They are needed to supplement the "management studies" of colleges and universities that focus on such matters as "mechanization of accounting and student records," "portion control of food served," "utilization of classroom space," and "elimination or reduction of maid service in dormitories."

As Logan Wilson has pointed out, it is high time that the college or university be "subjected to the same intensive analysis which has been brought to bear on various forms of business and industrial [and I would add, governmental] enterprise." [1] But that "intensive analysis" must distinguish the unique aspects of academic administration and the reasons for this uniqueness. It cannot conclude with unhelpful pontifications that governing boards should deal "with major matters and not with trivia," that "sound forward planning is essential," and that "effective and efficient internal management of a university's affairs depends upon the existence of sound organization." And, hence, answers are needed about the how and the why of the administrative process of a college or university.

The administration of any human enterprise—be it a military, religious, business, governmental, or educational enterprise—consists, as other students have demonstrated, of discernible, interrelated activities. [2] In summary, it has been contended that administration involves (1) the making of decisions which (2) are programed into a plan for implementation, (3) are communicated to all who must carry them out, (4) are controlled to ensure that they are carried out as programed, and (5) finally are appraised in the light of results and new conditions. [3] In what respects does the college or university carry on these five distinguishable administrative activities differently from the way the business firm or the governmental agency does, and why?

This question does *not* imply that the college or university should administer its affairs like the business firm or the governmental agency. Good administration is not necessarily reflected by a "smooth-running machine," nor by a no-nonsense, tightly coordinated system of activities. Good administration is better re-

[1] "A President's Perspective," in *Faculty-Administration Relationships*, report of a work conference sponsored by the Commission of Instruction and Evaluation of the American Council on Education, Washington, May 7–9, 1957.

[2] See, for example, the writings of Luther Gulick, Edward H. Litchfield, and Herbert A. Simon.

[3] Edward H. Litchfield, "Notes on a General Theory of Administration," *Administrative Science Quarterly*, June, 1956, pp. 3–29.

flected by a capacity to keep the eye focused on basic ends, to adapt activities to the attainment of these ends, and to ensure continual innovation. Our concern here is with the discovery of those environmental factors which condition how administrative activities in the university are carried on.

DIFFERENCES IN DECISION MAKING

Decision making, as has been emphasized, is the central and continual business of every human enterprise. How do the ways by which business firms, governmental agencies, and universities arrive at decisions differ?

Staff Guidance in Decision Making

For governmental agencies, purpose is usually set forth in legislation (e.g., to protect citizens against adulterated foods, drugs, and cosmetics) and is made more precise by periodic public review (e.g., citizens' advisory committees) and legislative review (e.g., annual appropriations hearings) of what the individual agency is doing. The public administrator often fails to translate the legislative purpose into precise guides for his staff. But an intelligible statement of purpose exists and frequently is made understood by the processes of public review.

For the employees of a manufacturing enterprise, purpose is set by the product produced (e.g., to manufacture paper products) and is made more precise by the reasonably apparent results in sales and profits. The manufacturer often reaffirms his purpose by a slogan ("comfort-conditioned") that gives internal direction even as it provides external identification. The newspaper publisher sets his purpose in terms of an editorial formula that gives direction to writers, editors, and others and tends to establish a distinctive character. The department-store owner strives to create a "public image" that identifies his store in customers' minds and guides employee dress, conduct, and sales talk, as well as the kind of merchandise stocked and the way in which it will be displayed and advertised. Notable illustrations of businesses that flounder because they lack a clear purpose confirm the importance of clearly stated purpose.

Less often does the multischooled university (or even the college) manifest a clear, generally understood purpose. Academic administrators generally agree that there is need for agreement about educational purpose to guide their allocation of limited resources. They seldom deny that the educational program, the curriculum, the kinds of student personnel services provided, the facilities provided for research, the plan for physical development, and the financial program all should be determined in terms of agreed-upon educational purpose.[4] But that they usually lack such a guiding purpose is attested to by most. For example, President A. Whitney Griswold of Yale University recently declared that the universities' "sense of purpose is all but smothered, their stated purposes blurred beyond recognition."[5]

The catalog will state a noble purpose in high-sounding terms. The chairman and president will speak of "service to youth." An "intuitive purpose" may reside in the minds of a few trustees, the president, and faculty members. But no explicit statement of purpose will be found in many colleges and universities for all to know and to follow in framing courses, curricula, student housing plans, or athletic programs; in determining what public services shall be undertaken; or particularly in allocating scarce resources among these several activities.

The significance of this lack is made all the more apparent by the success of institutions which have clearly defined and stead-

[4] For further development of this reasoning see Dewey B. Stuit, Gerald C. Helmstadter, and Norman Frederiksen, *Survey of College Evaluation Methods and Needs,* a report to the Carnegie Corporation, Educational Testing Service, Princeton, N.J., December, 1956, chap. 2, "Institutional Objectives."

[5] In an address at Johns Hopkins University, late 1958. See also Lloyd S. Woodburne, *Principles of College and University Administration,* Stanford University Press, Stanford, Calif., 1958, p. 145; and Robert M. Hutchins, "The Administrator," a paper delivered before the Summer Program for Federal Administrators, University of Chicago, 1958, in which he argued that ". . . the leading characteristic of educational institutions today is aimlessness."

fastly pursued a purpose.[6] Wesleyan's dedication to the liberal
arts [7] and California Institute of Technology's concentration on
the whole-sided training of scientists are but two illustrations; not
many could be added, though a clear and guiding but not domi-
nantly educational purpose guides many decisions in the national
military academies, some denominational schools, some junior colleges, and a few "athletic" universities.

Students of administration have long contended that a clear
guiding purpose is an essential to the effective administration of
any human enterprise. But enterprise concerned with the universality of knowledge and dedicated to the encouragement of inquiry
wherever it may lead exists in an environment in which the *precise*
definition of purpose is impossible. Forces within (students and
faculty) and without (alumni and constituencies) are given, or
take, substantial freedom in determining their own purpose. Yet
the trustees and presidents, consciously or unconsciously, do define
purpose or confuse their deans and department heads by the succession of decisions they make. In an enterprise where goals cannot
be clearly defined, the demand for leadership is large.[8]

Algo D. Henderson, formerly a college president and now director of the Center for the Study of Higher Education at the University of Michigan, has aptly summarized the significance of purpose to a university. In a letter to the author he states:

I have reflected upon the question whether the University of Michigan
has a purpose. In the broad sense it must have, for otherwise how could
it achieve such high distinction as a university. I doubt if this purpose is
expressed, and I haven't heard it mentioned in discussion. It seems to exist
as a "climate of learning."

[6] Paul H. Davis, former secretary of Stanford University and educational
consultant, after visiting many colleges concluded that the "best ones" (his
judgment, of course) are usually marked by a clear, universally accepted, and
relatively limited purpose.

[7] Victor L. Butterfield, *The Faith of a Liberal College,* the President's Annual
Report to the Board of Trustees, Wesleyan University, 1955.

[8] Philip Selznick, *Leadership in Administration,* Row, Peterson & Company,
Evanston, Ill., 1957, p. 16.

I am sure, however, that a president can engender new life and fresh vigor, can bind people together, by setting goals, making fresh interpretations of aims and stimulating new commitments. The magnetic effect is both internal and external.

In short, it is not the words of a statement of purpose that make for good administration. It is the existence of a defined purpose coupled with the leadership that brings about general understanding of such purpose and commitment to it.[9]

Diverging Interests and Loyalties of Faculty

An outstanding university president, when asked, "What is the prime purpose of your university?" replied, "It is impossible to state for an institution concerned with the universality of knowledge a single overriding purpose." Was he stating an axiom of university administration, or was he unconsciously complaining of the difficulty of welding the efforts of faculty members with widely varying interests and loyalties?

In business enterprises assurance that the individual will devote himself to the purpose of the enterprise is usually provided by his interest in continued employment and his identification of his own progress with the success of the enterprise. Instances during the late 1950s in which scientists in the atomic energy, aviation, and electronics industries left business firms to join others undertaking pioneer work in their fields of interest are so exceptional as to underline the customary assurance that the staff member's commitment is to the employing firm.

Perhaps it is somewhat more common for the political executives

[9] Wesleyan's stated purpose to serve as "a small college of liberal arts and sciences, independent and nonsectarian, committed in the Christian tradition to helping young men of outstanding mind and character grow in knowledge and wisdom, and in service to their fellow men" (President's Annual Report, 1955) is similar to the statements of many other colleges. The difference that marks Wesleyan lies in the extent to which trustees, academic officers, administrative officers, and faculty reflect understanding of and commitment to this purpose in their day-to-day actions. At Wesleyan common agreement on purpose, observation indicates, lends to the institution a unity and *esprit* that are evident at few other institutions.

of government agencies (and sometime the civil servants whose tenure is protected) to allow the interests of pressure groups (veterans, unions, or employers) or of political parties to influence their decisions. Yet those who have participated in the functioning of the Federal government will testify that such influences seldom guide responsible public officials (particularly the civil servants) to make decisions to the detriment of the agency they serve.

The university's decision-making process is complicated by the fact that most faculty members are attached to their disciplines (anthropology, geology, or zoology), or to the professions (architecture, law, or medicine) in which they are trained, much more intensely than either the business or the government employee seems to be attached to his program or functional specialty.[10] This commitment to discipline ahead of institution results in conflicts over courses, curriculum, and budgets. Moreover, the professor's "search for the truth" often makes difficult his objective weighing of alternatives and gives rise to conflicts with trustees and administrators over admissions, athletics, budgets, and building programs.

Focus of Responsibility in the Chief Executive and the Governing Board

In the business enterprise, decision making is usually focused in the chief executive. Though his decisions are reviewed and on major issues approved or vetoed by the board of directors, much authority is exercised by him alone. Similarly in government, the authority for decision making is clearly in the head of the agency.

In contrast, "under the prevailing governmental system and folklore of American higher education" many decisions about the basic program of the enterprise—admission of students, courses, curricula, and faculty, and often student affairs—are made by the faculty. "It is the privilege and the responsibility of the administration and trustees to mobilize and manage the physical and eco-

---

[10] One university vice president comments that "one learns well the attachment of the professor to his discipline or profession in reviewing faculty expense accounts; only his professional meeting will take him from home and the even tenor of his ways!"

nomic resources necessary to support the educational program which the faculty has determined."[11] And as institutions grow larger, the locus of decisions on courses, curricula, and faculty tends to slide down to the departmental faculty. Even the dean focuses his time and energy on matters of finance, buildings, and public relations.

The environmental cause of this diffusion of responsibility lies in the range and depth of specialization among the university's staff. "The professor," as Talcott Parsons has written, "is a technical expert who must take a heavy responsibility in an organization where his administrative superiors are almost always lacking in technical ability to evaluate the quality of his work."[12] The business or governmental executive, who is increasingly having to harness the efforts of technical and professional personnel, may find that the university president's wrestling with this problem charts his way.

The result of this diffusion and decentralization of decision making is often costly. Decisions by faculties regarding educational program are often the result of compromise among specialists, made without the leavening and stimulating influence of thoughtful leaders of the society who (sometimes) serve on boards of trustees.

The areas of decision making entrusted to faculties are in practice inseparable from those reserved for the president and trustees: the determination of the educational program or the establishment of admissions policy necessitates financial support, may also preclude increased expenditures for faculty salaries, and may require substantial additional facilities and the raising of funds. The president, when given only a limited opportunity to participate with the faculty in programing courses and curricula, is ill equipped to make informed decisions on matters of budget, fund raising, and the need for new capital expenditures.

Members of governing boards are frequently dissatisfied with

[11] Philip H. Coombs, director of research, Fund for the Advancement of Education, in a talk before the 14th National Conference on Higher Education, Association for Higher Education, Chicago, Mar. 3, 1959.

[12] "Suggestions for a Sociological Approach to the Theory of Organization—II," *Administrative Science Quarterly*, September, 1956.

their role, even while professing their realization that educational questions should be decided by the faculty. If trustees were permitted to participate more in educational decision making, their most important decision—the choice of a president—might be made better.

Captive "Consumers"

In private business a major influence over the decisions of an enterprise is the known or estimated views or tastes of the consumers of the product or service to be sold. Distributors of manufactured products regularly manifest, by their purchases, the views of consumers. Techniques of market research are steadily being improved to provide a surer reflection of consumer desires. And techniques designed to motivate consumers to want what they may not have wanted are being created!

In government the decisions of the enterprise are similarly influenced by the views and actions of the taxpayers, or by their representatives in the legislatures. Decisions reflect a continual awareness of the prospective reactions of such consumers. That awareness is guided by the representatives of taxpayers in the Congress, in the state legislatures, and in the municipal councils and the highly articulate pressure groups who reflect the wishes of the consumers of public services. And similarly improved techniques of public opinion research, and of more skilled political "soundings," give the public official a surer "feel" of the desires of his consumers to guide his decisions.

Academic officials, in contrast, have neither so forceful a reflection of consumer choice nor applied techniques of market research to guide their decisions on the kind of educational program to be offered. Obviously, some decisions are influenced by the reactions of students to courses of study,[13] to library services, and to regu-

---

[13] David Riesman suggests that innovations in educational program are sometimes resisted by students' tendency "to seek what might be called the higher vocationalism of the higher learning, and they have been attracted less by programs tailored to someone's definition of their life situation than by prestige." "Planning in Higher Education: Patterns and Problems," *Human Organization*, 18(1):16, spring, 1959.

lations about "cuts" or dormitories. Similarly, some decisions are influenced by the prospective reactions of parents who pay the bills and by the opinions of prospective employers. And more decisions are influenced by the desires of the "consumers"—government or business—who purchase research services. The contrast, and it is a substantial one, lies in the relative significance that faculty and administrators in the college or university attach to the consumers' view.

DIFFERENCES IN PLANNING AND PROGRAMING

Decisions better serve an enterprise, the foregoing has demonstrated, if they are guided by purpose. They will usually be better decisions if they can be preceded by some planning, i.e., thinking out what should be done. And to put a decision into effect requires the programing of a succession of actions. Here the term *programing* is used to describe these successive administrative processes.

In business the inextricable interrelationships of manufacturing, sales, advertising, finance, and other staffs impel programing, in more or less formal terms, so that each may understand what the other is doing. In governmental enterprises, similar interrelationships, e.g., between the regional and central offices of the National Labor Relations Board, tend to compel programing. It is also compelled by two other forces: the necessity of obtaining legislative sanction, usually in an appropriation, before many a decision can be carried out; and the fact that each public official may be called upon to explain, to the press or to citizen groups, what is being done and why.

In some academic institutions relatively formal and orderly programing has been impelled by the pressure of expanding enrollment and the necessity of planning the steps involved in a decision to expand.[14] Such a decision, for example, may necessitate an increase in size of faculty; in classrooms, laboratories, dormitories, dining rooms, library facilities, office space, and clerical staff.

[14] See, for a well-developed example, *A 15-Year Forecast of Students, Staff and Facilities for the University of Delaware*, Newark, 1958.

Course schedules may have to be modified. Simultaneously, a decision to expand enrollments may enable administrators and faculty to collaborate in reviewing ratios in each professorial rank, to reappraise the relative size of departments, to evaluate the effectiveness of particular academic units, and to determine which need strengthening in terms of staff. Such a decision may also permit raising salary schedules to facilitate competing for new staff in a time of expanding demand for services. Thus it will require planned action to determine how much financial support is needed and from what sources it will be raised.

But to a large degree neither the expansion nor the current operations of colleges and universities is guided by conscious thinking—and rethinking—out in advance of what is to be done, by whom, and when, i.e., by programing.[15] In most institutions, our observations suggest, both decisions to expand enrollment and decisions about expansion of the faculty, modification of curriculum, or the nature of student services to be provided are "taken as they come." This is not to say that the orderly thinking out and programing for what is to be done both in academic and operational activities is nonexistent among colleges and universities; it simply is to suggest that it is not common practice.

With respect to academic decisions two reasons seem apparent. First, the relatively complete (even if incongruous) separation of academic decision making by the faculty from economic de-

---

[15] David Riesman has declared that: "Certainly, research aimed at anticipating the long-run future is a more conspicuous feature of large corporations and of the armed services than even of large universities, although perhaps it would be fairer to say that such corporations and agencies are richer and more willing to pay for research (as part of the "conspicuous production" of a proper outfit) but are not always more willing to pay heed to it." *Op. cit.*, p. 13. He points out in a footnote to the same article that "ample evidence concerning lack of planning in personnel recruitment" by academic institutions is provided by Theodore Caplow and Reece McGee, *The Academic Marketplace*, Basic Books, Inc., New York, 1958. Finally, a 1958 survey by the management consultants Booz, Allen & Hamilton indicated that only 10 per cent of the colleges and universities had "adequate long range programs." Unfortunately, no comparable survey indicates whether the proportion of business enterprises having such programs would be significantly larger.

cision making by the president and trustees makes the programing of steps involving both difficult. Second, the lack of programing of academic decisions is attributable to the insistence of the academic man upon self-direction. The faculty member engages in group effort less often than his counterpart in business or in government; his teaching requires a more solitary type of effort.

COMMUNICATIONS—THE BLOOD STREAM OF HUMAN ENTERPRISE

Coordination and collaboration in any human enterprise, Barnard has written, is possible only when communication is effective.[16] Is this generalization equally applicable to business, government, and higher education?

In a manufacturing company decisions on the volume to be produced, the inventories needed, and the selling price all require some minimal horizontal communication among staffs engaged in purchasing, manufacturing, sales, advertising, and finance. Similarly, employees in the mail room, accounting units, auditing units, cashiers' cages, and the fields of a district office of the Internal Revenue Service must communicate, one with another, if personal income tax returns are to be processed on schedule.

Simultaneously, there is an accepted need for relaying orders from top executives down through both kinds of organization— private and public. And it is generally agreed that there is need for upward communication, from the man in the plant, the salesman, and the clerk to his superiors, even if such communication is not so regularly provided for and fostered.

Is it true that the members of a university faculty, to perform well their teaching and research functions, must continually interchange information and ideas with their colleagues and with the growing administrative staffs? Can it be assumed that there is need for the continual flow of "orders" and information from trustees, the president, and deans to faculty members and, in reverse, a flow of ideas and opinion from the faculty upward?

[16] Chester I. Barnard, *The Functions of the Executive,* Harvard University Press, Cambridge, Mass., 1938, p. 91.

President Litchfield of the University of Pittsburgh has implied affirmative answers in posing a series of related questions. He asks: [17]

Where is the institution in which all faculties enjoy regular and meaningful faculty meetings? Where is the large university which has found an even minimal procedure for systematically enabling one faculty to know what another is doing in fields of obviously mutual concern? Where is the institution in which trustees and administration views are regularly conveyed to the faculty, or in which faculty opinion is freely conveyed to the administration?

Most observers of college and university operations, and many participants in these operations, confirm Litchfield's views. In the institutions studied there were few exceptions to the generalization that the regular meetings of the general faculty did not provide meaningful discussions of significant problems of general interest. More meaningful were the meetings of school and departmental faculties, but in few instances were practices found which brought related faculties, e.g., the graduate school of business and the college department of economics, together for effective interchange.

Most presidents the author has encountered lament their inability to spend more time with their faculties. They meet from time to time with the university-wide faculty, but generally find such meetings useful only for the conduct of routine business and the making of announcements; they seldom find it feasible to use them for the exchange of opinion on policy questions. The president cannot get to the more numerous and more effective interchanges that take place in departmental and school faculty meetings. He may, and more often does, meet with a few key committees, usually those on educational policy, faculty personnel, and admissions. He finds this lack of effective contact with the faculty the more serious because he simultaneously lacks the primary channel of communication on which executives in other forms of en-

[17] *New Dimensions of Learning in a Free Society*, University of Pittsburgh Press, Pittsburgh, Pa., 1958, p. 287. A supplementary opinion is offered by George Winter, "Faculty-Trustee Communications," *AAUP Bulletin*, 42(4):620–623, 1956.

132   GOVERNANCE OF COLLEGES AND UNIVERSITIES

terprise depend: the hierarchical line of authority. The department heads (and sometimes deans)—scholars, not administrators, by training and bent—usually accept little responsibility for communication. They recognize an obligation to voice the views of their departmental colleagues to the deans and president, but do not regularly take the initiative in assembling those views and then presenting them to the administration. On the other hand, department heads less often recognize an obligation to translate positively to their colleagues the views of the president.

In most institutions there is little, if any, direct contact between trustees and the faculty. In principal part this is due to (1) the limited time trustees spend on the campus (they may meet monthly or quarterly and not infrequently off the campus) and (2) the insistence of the president upon being the conduit through which all communications shall flow.

There are notable exceptions. Throughout his tenure at Princeton, Harold Dodds encouraged periodic contact between trustees and faculty; regular dinner meetings were held at which faculty representatives described to members of a trustees' committee faculty plans and innovations. At Wesleyan a committee of the trustees (composed, it happens, of members of the board who are members of other university faculties) meets each year with the faculties of several departments and takes stock of departmental plans and reasoning; the meetings have met with a genuinely hospitable reception by the faculty. At Cornell four members of the faculty serve on the board of trustees.[18] In other institutions sporadic efforts to bring trustees and faculty members together are found. But in most institutions little effort is made to maintain direct and effective communication between trustees and faculty.

Four factors underlie the apparent lack of communication among faculties and between faculties and president and trustees. First and most important is the infinitely greater specialization among members of the university staff than is found in industry or government. Second, the individuality of thought typical of faculty

[18] The utility of this arrangement is vigorously questioned by F. G. Marcham in an article entitled "Faculty Representation on the Board of Trustees," *AAUP Bulletin*, 42(4):617–619, 1956.

members poses special problems for communication. Third, the hierarchy of deans and department heads in many institutions cannot be directed to communicate and interpret to the faculty as the foremen and division heads in business can be ordered to pass the word along. Fourth, confusion generally prevails about what matters should be communicated to all on the faculty, e.g., is it useful or wasteful to inform the professor of history on the cost of a new furnace, and should he be asked to offer an opinion on whether a new furnace shall be installed?

In summary, these factors make difficult the establishment of a broad context of understandings that welds faculty and staff into dynamic collaboration in creating an enriched educational environment.

CONTROL—SEEING THAT ACTION IS TAKEN

A principal task of management is to receive information, to compare this information with some ideal, and to issue orders which it believes will make the enterprise more effective. This task, in the jargon of management, is called *control*—a nasty word in any self-respecting academic community.

The performance of workers in the factory, for example, is appraised in standard unit costs for each operation as well as in quality. The salesman's accomplishments are measured in relation to a sales goal set for his division. In short, the performance of each aspect of the well-managed business enterprise is regularly reviewed against some standards.

Employees engaged in many activities in government are similarly "controlled." The chemist in a public health laboratory may be expected to handle, on the average, an established number of analyses. The adjudicator in a regional office of the Veterans Administration may be evaluated in terms of number of claims handled. The clerk in a military matériel center may be expected to complete a stipulated number of procurements per day. The executive must assess likely public reaction and judge what is sound public policy in deciding major questions, but the assessment and judgment will be aided by data about work to be done and the capacity of employees to accomplish that work.

Standards, usually in terms of cost, are emerging for a number of the university's nonacademic functions.[19] For example, standards are set for the maintenance of buildings and grounds, the operation of dormitories and dining rooms, and even the operation of the library. Standards are being developed by which administrators can control the utilization of classrooms.[20] Similarly, the performance of alumni, friends, and faculty in the development campaign is measured against preestablished goals. And even the performance of teachers is partially evaluated by the slide rule when the number of "student credit hours per full-time faculty equivalent" or similar measures are used in arriving at decisions.

For many kinds of activities and personal performances in business, in government, and especially in universities, control in such a mechanistic sense is not feasible. The accomplishment of the development engineer in the industrial plant, of the financial executive of the manufacturing company, of the general counsel of a major Federal agency, or of the deputy director of the Bureau of the Budget cannot be appraised by tangible standards.

In the university, decisions on curriculum, faculty selection and promotion, admissions, budgets, and even buildings must, in the final analysis, be based on judgment about what will contribute most to the influencing of attitudes and values of young men and women or to discovery of new knowledge. The essential activity of universities takes place in the minds of men—the ideas produced by the scholar's intellect and their communication to the minds of students are not susceptible to comparison with fixed standards.

[19] For example, see A Study of Income and Expenditures in Sixty Colleges—Year 1953–54 (1955) and The Sixty College Study—A Second Look (1960), both compiled and published under the direction of the National Federation of College and University Business Officers Associations.

[20] For illustrations see Rollin E. Godfrey, The Role of the Registrar in Institutional Research, The Woman's College of the University of North Carolina, July, 1959; and Institutional Research Concerning Land Grant Institutions and State Universities, a report prepared by W. Hugh Stickler for the Joint Office of Institutional Research of the Association of Land Grant Colleges and State Universities and the State Universities Association, September, 1959, appendix D.

To assess the teacher on the basis of teaching load, grade curves, number of theses directed, number of papers published, and like measures is to place undue emphasis on the insignificant in his job. But this judgment can be aided by the assembly of pertinent data. And among American institutions of higher education there is a growing movement to identify and develop those operational statistics which will permit the president and his principal academic officers to be better informed about the character of educational programs and operations. The American Council on Education endeavored during 1957 to 1959 to stimulate this activity among colleges and universities. Offices of "institutional research" have been established at a number of institutions regularly to collect the kinds of data outlined. In addition, and most usefully, these offices have been exploring what additional data would reveal for administrators the effectiveness and status of each facet of institutional operations. Thus these offices enable presidents (and their staffs) to review with deans and department heads, objectively and more effectively, the adequacy of facilities, the teaching loads borne by faculty members, the instructional needs of students, the effectiveness of student personnel services, and the effectiveness of instruction.

But the directors of offices of institutional research, as well as administrators, recognize that as the level of intellectual effort required for a task rises, the applicability of precise standards as a basis for evaluation has less and less meaning. The administrator and the professional man in business, in government, and in the university are controlled, in major part, by continuing *self*-appraisal. Only the teacher's conscience really appraises the changes in critical thinking, in attitudes, in appreciation, and in related skills that are induced by his teaching. Only his specialist colleagues can judge the quality and importance of his research. And it is doubtful whether the efforts of the administrator or the professional man would be stimulated by tangible standards against which their performance could be appraised.

The university administrator—president, dean, or department head—does not need (and would not be allowed to use) tangible standards with which to control the performance of faculty members. Most faculty members are sensitive both to student opinion and to the evaluation of their colleagues. What the university administrator needs is the capacity to lead his faculty in a continuing quest for agreement on improved methods of teaching, counseling, and research that will induce each faculty member to strive to improve his own performance. And in this respect the task of the university administrator is quite similar to that of the business or the governmental executive in stimulating the performance of scientific workers and executives.

PROCESSES FOR TAKING STOCK

In business and often in government there are numerous built-in devices for appraisal of the product, the process, and the individual. Such appraisal propels the agency forward and has therapeutic value for the individual whose contribution to the corporate effort is evaluated.

In business the customer continually appraises the product and gives his verdict in a telling manner. The annual profit and loss statement appraises the over-all performance of the enterprise and frequently is broken down to measure the results achieved by plants and divisions. These built-in devices are supplemented by staff agencies, e.g., the comptroller, the quality control staff, or the chief engineer, who appraise the product in terms of standards and customer complaints and the process in terms of cost and method. Finally, the performance of individuals is evaluated against sales goals, work standards, or the judgment of superiors. Appraisal is an integral, accepted part of the process of administration.

The reaction of the customer is not necessarily influential in telling the public executive the worth of his service, but taxpayers and voters do have ways of expressing their judgments. There is no equally succinct and precise substitute in government for the over-all appraisal offered by the profit and loss statement, but the legislative appropriations committee does hold the agency, its program, and its performance up to the light. Staff agencies similarly appraise method, but are not aided by as readily available unit cost data.

In the administration of the university, appraisal processes are less often built in. The "customers," i.e., the students, are by and large submissive and inarticulate in expressing judgments on the intellectual fare they are fed. The chief executive has no periodical over-all measure of accomplishments. Some universities and a few colleges have staff agencies to assemble data that will aid academic officers to reach better-informed judgments about the accomplishments or even the burdens borne by each department and school,[21] but the proportion is very small.

More important, there is less acceptance of the need for regular reappraisal either of educational product or of teaching. Faculty members, like counterparts in industry and in government, manifest a resistance to change—in courses, curricula, programs, and teaching methods. Innovation, that fragile but vital force for progress in any human enterprise, finds tough going in the typical university.[22]

Appraisal of Program

With few tools for appraisal and with limited acknowledgment of his right to appraise, the president or dean cannot know the educational program for which he must seek support, nor can he effectively lead in its improvement. Moreover, he has only impressions on whether classrooms, laboratories, and dormitories are effectively utilized or the library efficiently run. To aid in appraising operations, three devices are used occasionally:

Visiting Committees. In a few institutions academic officers are aided by visiting committees, serving essentially as their tools in measuring performance. Customarily this term *visiting committee* is applied to a group of specialists in the subject matter of the school or department to be evaluated, i.e., businessmen, lawyers, engineers, or public administrators, who come in from outside

---

[21] See Godfrey, *op. cit.*, for discussion of the operation analyses carried on in fifty-three colleges and universities.

[22] In part because the chief executive, who in any form of large enterprise is expected to supply ideas for or to stimulate innovation, in the university often avoids the contribution or stimulation of ideas to avoid the risk of conflict or disharmony. For similar view, see Riesman, *op. cit.*

to evaluate accomplishments and plans. The visiting committees of the Harvard Board of Overseers constitute one of the best-known examples. In a few institutions, e.g., the University of Chicago and Wesleyan University, the president is aided by committees of trustees who study and appraise a particular activity or school. Unfortunately, there is substantial question about the value of visiting committees, and there is little orderly analysis of their use on which to evaluate their contribution to the appraisal process.

Accreditation. Many presidents would deny that the appraisal of the accrediting association aids them! Yet both general and professional accrediting associations, e.g., the American Council on Engineering Education, regularly inspect or stimulate the faculty to inspect the educational program of the whole institution or of a school or department. Indeed, one president has complained that "our chemistry department is more thoroughly appraised than anything in modern government, business, or the Air Force!" And such inspections or "self-studies" do provoke questions for consideration and provide facts on which appraisal is founded.

Management Studies. Perhaps 200 colleges and universities within this decade retained management consultants to study problems of organization, purchasing, finance, buildings, and grounds. Together these two—the self-study of educational program and processes by the faculty and the study of administrative matters by outside consultants—have not added up to an effective appraisal of the *whole* institution. What is needed is a fusion of the two that gives to trustees, president, deans, and faculty a whole-sided appraisal of the university, rather than of its parts.[23]

Appraisal of Teaching. Above all, there is need for appraisal of the performance of the individual. If there is a lack of recurring and comprehensive appraisal of educational product and of process, there is manifestly greater lack of appraisal of the individuals who day by day translate this program into reality—the faculty members.[24]

---

[23] Coombs, *op. cit.*

[24] Ralph W. Tyler, director, Center for Advanced Study in the Behavioral Sciences, Palo Alto, Calif., and an experienced teacher and academic administrator, has written: "Sound and systematic evaluation of college teaching is exceedingly

At Princeton the preceptor system of instruction, long in use there, brings teachers together to plan and evaluate their individual teaching and results in a continuing cross-appraisal of performance, particularly of the younger members of the faculty by a senior professor. At Wesleyan there is a continuing interchange of ideas among a relatively small and alert faculty as to how teaching methods can be improved. In a number of institutions the procedure by which a department head recommends a faculty member for promotion requires the expression of a judgment on the individual's "general effectiveness as a teacher." At both Oberlin and Reed colleges, for example, the procedure is firmly established, forms are regularly filled out, and appropriate faculty committees—and then academic officers—weigh the appraisals made by the department head. At the University of Washington an even more elaborate system of appraisal has been used. An evaluation committee of seven people rates each individual who is recommended for promotion or to acquire tenure; nine items are used, one of which is "teaching effectiveness."

At most institutions instructors and assistant professors expect some appraisal by senior members of their departments. Yet the evidence indicates that there is a prevailing question about the willingness or ability of academic officers or colleagues to evaluate the teaching of another. They insist that one teacher (or department head or dean) is never privileged to invade the classroom of another to evaluate his teaching.

REASONS FOR RARITY OF APPRAISAL

Two basic reasons account for the lack or ineffectiveness of processes for the appraisal of teachers:

1. Confusion prevails about what is expected of the teacher. Is he expected to concentrate on teaching? Must he publish the results of research? What proportion of his time should be given to administrative chores? [25]

rare and yet it is highly essential to the improvement of college instruction."
In a privately circulated paper entitled *The Evaluation of Teaching.*

[25] Logan Wilson wrote: "In view of the vague and conflicting criteria by

2. The notion prevails at most institutions (and there are notable exceptions, like Oberlin and Reed) that one cannot evaluate the teaching of another, and that a department head or dean is never privileged to invade the classroom of an individual who has reached professorial rank.

Yet teaching *is* appraised. Students tell their contemporaries of the strengths and weaknesses of the teacher and sometimes express themselves candidly to their faculty advisers or to the dean. More substantially, each faculty member is appraised whenever some are promoted in salary or status and others are not.

The difficulty is that the constructive value of appraisal is lost because no agreed-upon standards exist and the utility of appraisal is not accepted. The concept that a superior (e.g., the department head) is responsible for the growth of his colleagues (e.g., the associate and full professors) has great vogue in business and government, but is effectively abandoned in education after the teacher reaches tenure rank, if not before. Appraisal, the foundation of development, actually continues in the university setting, but the appraisers themselves deny their ability or right to make such appraisals!

At a number of universities, offices of institutional research are accumulating data and devising means by which the administrator can better understand, if not appraise, the product, program, process, and performance of the teacher for which he has a measure of responsibility. The task these offices have commenced upon is as difficult as it is important. It is made difficult by the diversity of function; that is, the wide range of disciplines within which faculty members are continually at work makes difficult the establishment of measures generally useful for appraisal of the performance of individuals working in each. The intangibility of the product—influence over the mind and the attitudes of the students—intensifies the difficulty of appraising what either the educational program or the faculty's teaching has accomplished. The insulation of the

which his work is judged, he is uncertain in the allocation of his energies. He knows that he is a competitor, but often is not clear regarding the terms of the competition." *The Academic Man*, Oxford University Press, New York, 1942, p. 62.

disciplines, one department from another, and even of the specialists within a discipline, challenges the capacity of the dean or
department head to appraise the performance of those who serve
on the faculties over which these academic officers preside. In short,
the administrator's task in the university is made infinitely more
difficult than the task of his counterpart in business or in government not only by the lack of built-in means of appraisal, but by
the complexity of developing such measures.

CONTRASTING ADMINISTRATIVE PROCESSES

An assumption underlies all that has preceded. It is that if the
sum total of the efforts of human beings working together in the
corporation, in public service, in military organizations, or in educational institutions is to be fully effective, the group will utilize
a common administrative process.

The processes by which a president or a dean gets things done
through a faculty differ from those by which a business executive
or a governmental official customarily goes about his work. The
academic administrator requires equal imagination and capacity
to analyze, and greater patience and skills of persuasion to lead
faculty members—and oftentimes trustees—in making decisions
for which authority is theirs, and not his. The influence of govern-
ing-board members in the university is limited in a way unknown
to the business director (or the legislative oversight committee in
government); trustees generally refrain meticulously from expressing judgments on the substance of the educational program. The
faculty is granted, by practice and tradition, a greater role in the
governance of the university than are its counterparts in business or
in government.

When one takes into account the context within which this institution functions, he will recognize six underlying and interrelated factors which account for the differences in administrative
processes that obtain:

1. The university's goals are not clearly defined and are comprehensive in character; they provide no specific guiding purpose;

they give great opportunity for free play to faculty members and place large demands for leadership on presidents, deans, and department heads.

2. The product or service that the university produces is less tangible than that of many other enterprises.

3. The customers, that is, the students or their prospective employers, exercise limited influence upon the judgment of those who participate in making the decisions of the enterprise.

4. The faculty is made up of individuals who are highly specialized in many fields; most of them are committed intellectually and careerwise to a discipline or profession rather than to the employing university.

5. Like professionals in other enterprises, they expect the right of self-direction in their work, and the opportunity to participate in decisions that generally affect the conditions under which they work.

6. The right to participate in the making of decisions is diffused among a greater proportion of the participants in the enterprise than is typical of other forms of organization.

Much remains for other students to determine about how the most successful universities have achieved effective and dynamic group effort—good administration. The success of their inquiries will be directly related to their recognition of, and ability to analyze imaginatively, the context within which universities operate and have their being.

Chapter 7

THE ECOLOGY OF GOVERNANCE

CONTINUAL ADJUSTMENT—INSTITUTIONS AND SOCIETY

"IF THE COLLEGE were wholly alien to its environment," Henry Wriston has written, "it could not perform its function. . . . On the other hand, if it yields completely to its environment, it equally fails in its objectives. It must maintain a realistic contact without compromising its essential function." [1]

Previous chapters have defined the college's "essential function": to translate the talents and capabilities of a faculty into significant educational results. They have also described the respective roles that trustees, the president and his aides, the academic officers, and the faculty play in the making of decisions which constitute the governance of their respective institutions. By what forces or groups within the environment are these several participants in the decision-making process influenced?

American education, and especially higher education, has been subjected for many decades to the pressures of groups that would have it modify its program, its processes, or in some instances the views its teachers hold. The purpose of this chapter is to consider the nature of such pressures [2] as they are manifested within the college or university. The groups which usually exert such pressures

[1] Henry M. Wriston, *The Nature of the Liberal Arts College*, Lawrence College Press, Appleton, Wis., 1937, p. 20.

[2] The term *pressures* is *not* used in this chapter to connote the effort of a group to have the institution distort its program, its action, or the views of

143

are alumni, contractors for research, churches and religious bodies, governmental agencies, professional associations, accrediting organizations, donors (individual and corporate), and the general public. No attempt is made here to dissect in precise terms the objectives and influence of each of these groups. Here it is only proposed to indicate the nature of these pressures and, thus, to illustrate an important influence that affects the governance of American colleges and universities.

THE DIVERSITY OF ALUMNI INFLUENCE

The very personal relationship of the graduate to his or her alma mater is an apparent characteristic of American higher education. "The alumni of American colleges and universities never cease to think of themselves as members of the family," former president Robert G. Sproul of the University of California has commented.[3] President Sproul referred to this "family" relationship as "vital" and spoke of the benefits accruing to the institution as a result of the loyal affection of alumni. At least in the privacy of their own studies, and in moments of discouragement, other presidents, while recognizing this family relationship, have spoken of the handicaps, rather than benefits, which alumni impose upon their alma mater.[4]

That alumni do have, or can be stimulated to have, a continuing interest in the institutions that they attended is readily apparent. The problem of administration is: How can this interest be built upon and channeled to the greatest good of the institution?

That it has been effectively stimulated and channeled into increasing the financial support of many institutions is a matter

individuals in order to serve the selfish interests of the group. The pressure may be a constructive force, stimulating the institution's advance.

[3] From "Responsibilities of Alumni for Quality in Education," by Theodore A. Distler, in *1955 Yearbook,* American Alumni Council, Washington.

[4] Consider the ruminations of the fictional president of Rowley University in the engaging novel by Theodore Morrison, *The Stones of the House,* The Viking Press, Inc., New York, 1953. President Andrew Aiken battled valiantly against the insistence of the mobilized alumni that land required for a much needed library should be reserved for a new fraternity house.

of record. In 1957–1958, the American Alumni Council reports, alumni contributed more than $140 million. They provide a continuing and increasingly important source of support. For public institutions, they also support requests to legislatures and to city councils for more generous financing.

That it has been effectively stimulated and channeled into non-educational interests has been apparent in many institutions. Alumni support of the football team is traditional; it is also substantial in terms of the funds contributed, usually through non-institutional channels, for the support of athletes. The football coach earns his pay, in today's competition, as much by his ability to marshal the ardent and tangible support of alumni, as by his work on the field or in recruiting athletes.

But the stereotype of the vociferous alumnus, rampant in support of the college football team or intent on retaining "Old Main" as a campus structure, is a limited or even distorted concept of alumni-institutional relations today in many institutions. Unquestionably, many alumni eye their alma mater in the image of their undergraduate days, especially athletics, and resist change in the landmarks and the practices they look back to with pleasure.

Woodrow Wilson faced such resistance when he sought to eliminate the social clubs at Princeton. Stanford University administrators, the president of the University of Virginia, the president of Randolph-Macon Woman's College, and others have met similar opposition when they raised questions about the role of fraternities or sororities in campus life. More than one president has felt the threat of successful but conservatively minded alumni to cut off potential donations because of faculty attitudes or activities. Yet, during recent years more serious alumni concern with the educational objectives and functioning of colleges and universities has been stimulated and developed in a limited number of institutions.

The administrative task of channeling the interest and effort of alumni has to be focused both on alumni as individuals and on the organized alumni. The task is a single one, but the methods and arrangements for each approach are different and require attention.

146   GOVERNANCE OF COLLEGES AND UNIVERSITIES

As individuals, alumni are of a wide variety. They are parents of today's students, leaders in business or in the professions, or potential donors, and among them are held many shades of opinion. Some are interested in particular intellectual fields, let us say graduate business administration, and can be induced to marshal the support of fellow businessmen in the institution's work in this field; others are journalists and can be looked to to promote the institution's interests through their writings and through their interest in the institution's work in this field. Some will condemn individual faculty expressions of strong views on public issues; others will applaud the same views.[5]

Some will willingly serve as the recruiters (not necessarily of athletes!) and will work diligently to encourage first-rate students to enroll in their alma mater. Others will work as diligently to place graduates and to serve as volunteer fund solicitors or as members of special committees to undertake tasks that the administration may require be done; and others can be induced to serve in a variety of roles. A few return for postbaccalaureate or postprofessional study, especially to the urban universities. Some look to their institutions for continuing intellectual stimulation, and a few alumni journals now devote space to consideration of serious educational issues, e.g., the Columbia University alumni journal has become an organ for intellectual discussion.

The influence of such individuals on internal decision making varies substantially. Presidents facing annual budget deficits cannot forget the alumni who donate either in small or in large amounts. Those alumni, like other donors, who give in generous amounts exercise a personal influence on general policy and frequently, with their donations, favor one aspect of an institution's program, e.g., a stadium, a field house, a library, or a professional school, over others. The alumni whose interests run to a particular

5 E. M. Hopkins, former president, is reported to have said at the time of the Sacco-Vanzetti case that one alumnus cut Dartmouth out of his will because a pro-Sacco-Vanzetti professor had not been fired, and another took similar action because permission was denied to hold a pro-Sacco-Vanzetti meeting in a college hall!

school or department may have a major and sometimes unrecognized influence on the program of that school or department. The alumni who advise fraternities or sororities exercise direct influence on internal student affairs and student-institutional relations. The alumnus who follows the athletic team and frequents the locker room exerts influence. All of these actions of individual alumni total up to a substantial influence that needs to be recognized and channeled to the institution's good.

At the same time, the alumni of most institutions are organized into formal alumni groups. These vary from local associations of interested alumni in a region or a city to nation-wide associations of local chapters headed by elected presidents and by formal alumni councils constituted of selected or elected representatives who meet regularly to consider both alumni and other institutional affairs. The presidents or heads of these formal bodies often assume an important—whether official or unofficial—status with administration. Such councils serve to organize alumni interest in the college or university and to assist its administrators with whatever objectives, programs or campaigns for fund raising, student recruitment, and other institutional activities that they may choose or may be induced to support.

An increasing number of institutions have members of their governing boards elected or selected by alumni or alumni councils. Thus, Stanford University now has 3 elected alumni trustees. At Princeton University, 8 of 42 trustees are selected by alumni. Many other universities and colleges, by tradition, have boards composed substantially of alumni. The degree to which and the manner in which alumni so involved affect decisions warrant more considered investigation by students of college and university administration than they have yet received. Under what circumstances, for example, and under what arrangements does board membership by alumni lead to better understanding and support of basic educational objectives among "organized alumni"? How can broad-gauged leaders among the alumni be obtained as board members while still ensuring effective representation of organized alumni?

Alumni, experience makes clear, cannot be disregarded, either as individuals or as an organized group. Hence, the obvious trend among universities, as pictured by the American Alumni Council, is to give greater recognition to the organized alumni, to seek to associate interested alumni with the organized groups, and to interest the organized alumni in an increasingly broader assortment of the institution's activities. Studies by the American Alumni Council indicate that the official presidential door is being opened wider to the alumni point of view. Alumni secretaries have become, increasingly, members of the presidential staff, rather than agents of "his majesty's loyal opposition." Increasingly, offices and clerical staffs are being provided by the universities and the colleges rather than being financed by alumni dues or contributions.[6]

Harold Stoke, an experienced college president, questions whether administrators do not overrate the influence of alumni. He writes: [7]

Just how much is an active alumni organization worth to a college or university? It is a nice question, and there will be outrage and horror in some quarters at the suggestion that it is worth much less than is usually thought. The value, of course, varies widely as between types of schools, the uses made of alumni and the aggressiveness of alumni interest.

Realistically, Stoke misses the question. If alumni, as Sproul has contended, consider themselves as members of the institutional family and continue to manifest an interest in one phase of the institution's life or another, and if, as is increasingly apparent, college and university administrators increasingly need the support of alumni—financially, public relations-wise, and morally—then the question is: How can the influence of alumni be stimulated and

---

[6] To be effective, it is pointed out, alumni secretaries need two hats—one under which they represent the administration to the alumni, the other under which they represent the alumni to the administration. They cannot serve, in effect, as simply a university employee or public relations agent.

In this connection, Ohio State University has inaugurated by trustee action a formal alumni advisory board which serves to represent alumni thought in university operations. John B. Fullen, "The Alumni Secretaries: Men or Mites?" *American Alumni Council News*, February-March, 1956, p. 14.

[7] *The American College President*, Harper & Brothers, New York, 1959, p. 97.

channeled into directions that will further the total good of the institution?

A NEW INFLUENCE—CONTRACTUAL RESEARCH

A report of The Council of State Governments lists the "enormous expansion of research activities of higher education" as one of the most significant developments of the last twenty years.[8] Prior to World War II, faculty members carried out relatively modest projects, often without financial aid or with small foundation grants, or as part of the Federally supported activities of the land-grant colleges. Since 1939–1940 the aggregate sum spent for university research has increased from about $42 million, or about 8 per cent of the total national budget for higher education, to approximately $831 million, or 22 per cent of the total 1958–1959 budget.[9] The bulk of this increase in available funds has come from the Federal government (perhaps $450 million in 1958–1959), but substantial sums have been provided by industry as well.

The result is an increasing dependence on these monies. Once committed to an extensive program of contractual research, universities find it difficult indeed to withdraw from or reduce this activity. And the university administrator is confronted with impelling pressures which materially influence important institutional decisions.[10]

[8] The report reads: "Here, again, statistical data are incomplete at best. For the most part, only those research projects which are budgeted separately are reported by the Office of Education under the expenditure classification 'research.' Even so, the research expenditures it reports multiplied 12.5 times, from $18 million in 1930 to $225 million in 1950." *Higher Education in the Forty-eight States,* The Council of State Governments, Chicago, Ill., 1952, p. 70. See also John C. Weaver, "What Federal Funds Mean to the Universities Today," *The Annals,* American Academy of Political and Social Science, 327:114–122, January, 1960.

[9] C. C. Furnas and Raymond Ewell, "The Role of Research in the Economics of Universities," chap. 4 in Dexter M. Keezer (ed.), *Financing Higher Education: 1960–1970,* McGraw-Hill Book Company, Inc., New York, 1959, p. 94.

[10] A recent University of California faculty conference report lists a number of ways in which grants of research funds affect both the scholarship and the

Decisions Regarding Curriculum

The substantial financial support available for research makes difficult the administrators' task of ensuring balanced curricular offerings. The research interests of a scholar will, almost inevitably, result in the inclusion of a course in the department's offerings. A collection of such courses may not adequately serve the bulk of the student body who do not plan scholarly careers and whose education requires a broader grasp of the world's knowledge.[11] Moreover, the prospect of publication or of advancement in his field through significant research results will often incline a professor to neglect teaching, particularly of undergraduates, in favor of research.

Decisions Regarding Faculty Membership

The prestige of research enters into decisions regarding the employment of new staff. Colleges and universities lacking facilities and opportunities for contractual research, especially in the sciences, find it difficult to attract scholars of repute or even beginning scholars. On the other hand, colleges and universities with established research programs will attract new faculty members with proved research capabilities and will favor them over men with teaching capabilities. In the long run, this will tend to reinforce the prestige of major institutions [12] and make difficult the development of research in other institutions.

---

teaching of a major university. *University of California: Retrospect and Prospect*, Berkeley, Calif., 1958, pp. 49–54.

[11] It cannot be denied that the general education movement has spread even while the funds available for research have been multiplied.

[12] Faced with this problem and concerned with maintaining an atmosphere of scholarly inquiry to help maintain teaching creativity, administrators in smaller universities and colleges might well consider favoring a different kind of scholarship. The high degree of specialization in research suggests the need for academic endeavor concerned with what W. H. Cowley has described as "democentric teaching." In an address before the Institute of College and University Administrators meeting at Harvard University, June 20–29, 1960, he advocated that some teachers concentrate on organizing facts and concepts as a foundation for teaching the citizen rather than the specialist.

Decisions Regarding Facilities and Budgets

Research now consumes more than one-quarter of the total annual budget of a number of this country's major universities.[13] The administrators of these (and other institutions with lesser expenditures for research) are continually confronted with two demanding financial problems:

The Allocation Problem. The large sums required to provide the laboratories and equipment needed to support research programs tend to warp the budget to favor certain subject-matter areas, e.g., the physical sciences in preference to the humanities.

The "Short Fall" Problem. Federal grantor agencies fail to meet the total costs of the research that they stimulate. Their contracts fail to bear adequately the costs of university administration and operation, in addition to the specific costs of research projects. Thus such research reduces the resources from which the universities must support all activities.

Decisions Regarding Institutional Function

A total of about seventy-five universities does virtually all of the research done by this country's universities.[14] Both governmental and industrial agencies favor these universities in making contracts or grants for research. These institutions, hence, are able to attract the best graduate students and are enabled to strengthen and to expand their already substantial advantages.

Some, if not all, of these institutions are confronted with these questions: How much research is too much? When the institution's research program includes major laboratories or research centers divorced from the university's teaching, does the program form a logical part of the university's function?

Such questions arise in the universities that operate the twenty-eight Federal research centers under contracts with the Department of Defense or the Atomic Energy Commission, e.g., Electronics Research Laboratory, Stanford University; Human Resources Research Office, George Washington University. The

[13] *Sponsored Research Policy*, A Report of the Committee on Research Policy, American Council on Education, 1954, p. 30.

[14] Furnas and Ewell, *op. cit.*, p. 100.

operation of such centers poses large budgetary and managerial problems. In three universities, each of which operates three or four centers, research expenditures equal half or more of the total annual budget. There, and in some universities with lesser expenditures for research, the administrator must make trying decisions if he is to maintain balance between research and other activities.

In these universities, too, the management of large laboratories (e.g., the Jet Propulsion Laboratory at the California Institute of Technology employed more than 2,500 employees as of January 1, 1960) poses for president and governing board complex problems not integral to the management of the university. If these officials devote adequate time and attention to managing the center, they are unable to give as fully of their energies to the university's central activities; if they delegate very broad responsibilities to those who manage these laboratories and give little time and attention to their supervision, one wonders what contribution the university makes as the contractor—other than lending its name to a remotely associated activity.

Over-all Impact on Decisions

Contractual research, in short, can shape the destiny of a university without regard to what its administrators and faculty believe its appropriate function to be. A broadly balanced research program stimulates faculty growth, attracts good graduate students, and helps to keep the institution attuned to the needs of contemporary society. But research can consume faculty time needed for undergraduate teaching; the effort to produce research scientists can dissipate resources also needed to educate men in other professions and as citizens; [15] the prestige of investigation can overshadow the importance of good teaching (even in institutions concentrating on teaching, the research scholar may enjoy greater prestige than his colleague who concentrates on teaching).

[15] See, for example, P. E. Klopsteg, "Role of Government in Basic Research," *Science*, 121:781–784, June 3, 1955, p. 782; and Weaver, *op. cit.*, pp. 119–120.

THE INFLUENCE OF GOVERNMENTS

For over a century government (Federal, state and local) has been an increasing source of support for higher education. In recent decades it has been a major source of funds for public institutions and a growing source of revenue for private ones. Even if tuition charges are raised substantially and philanthropy increases its contributions, more than a doubling of governmental support . . . will be required to accommodate growing enrollments, increase salaries, and maintain or improve instruction.[16]

The availability of this substantial financial support, the manner in which it is made available, and the controls that are exercised over receiving institutions all influence the decisions made by those who run both public and private institutions. Five major kinds of influence deserve consideration.

Supervision

Government—Federal or state—has traditionally exercised little or no control over the academic standards or affairs of both private and public colleges and universities. The governing boards of private institutions are chartered by the state. The boards of state and municipal institutions are established in law and their members appointed by public officials. Yet, throughout the years most boards have been permitted to manage the institutions over which they preside with little interference or even review of their decisions.[17]

During recent decades, as the number of state-supported institutions has grown and their expenditures have increased, there has been a persistent tendency to establish means of coordination. In some states, e.g., California and Minnesota, this has taken the form of a central board with some authority for coordination over the state colleges and universities, each of which has its own board.

[16] Robert D. Calkins, "Government Support of Higher Education," chap. 9 in *Financing Higher Education: 1960–1970*, p. 183.

[17] There have been exceptions. For instance, a Florida governor blocked the appointment of a president elected by the board by threatening to withhold the payment of his salary.

In other states, e.g., Indiana and Ohio, coordination has been sought
by voluntary agreement among the institutions. In still other
states, e.g., North Carolina and Texas, master boards with operational control over the state's institutions of higher education have
been established.[18]

The impact of such coordinative agencies upon the authority of
governing boards and presidents of state institutions varies from
state to state, and institution to institution. But the existence of
this external influence for public institutions is generally apparent.
Of this kind of oversight, private institutional administrators are
free.

Another type of state supervision, that which has to do with
the licensing of various practitioners that serve the public, however, affects the decisions of the executives of both public and private institutions. By the requirements and processes established
for the admission to practice or certification of lawyers, doctors,
teachers, nurses, and public accountants, the state materially influences the curricula that each institution must offer. Similarly,
state requirements for employment in a variety of state services,
e.g., in agriculture, forestry, law enforcement, and welfare agencies, influence the educational programs offered by both public
and private institutions.

Direct Support

For public colleges and universities the prime source of support
is direct appropriations by the state governments. In addition the
land-grant colleges receive Federal aid. Over and above these substantial sources of support, both public and private institutions
derive support from the reserve officers training programs, grants
and contracts for medical education, grants and contracts for
research, surplus property, and Federal loans for the construction
of college buildings. Finally, the Federal government sends employees to universities for special training, offers scholarships and

[18] For an excellent discussion of the emergence of such state coordinating
efforts see Malcolm Moos and Francis E. Rourke, *The Campus and the State,* Johns
Hopkins Press, Baltimore, 1959, chap. 9, pp. 203–226.

fellowships in several fields (atomic energy and public health, where trained manpower is critically needed), and offers student loans and graduate fellowships in a wide range of fields under the National Defense Education Act.

Despite its substantial increase there is little evidence that Federal and state support is accompanied by the imposition by public officials of authority over educational policies, personnel, and practices. Yet the very availability of these funds does influence internal decision making. The availability of funds for some purposes (e.g., medical education) and for scholarships in some fields (e.g., science training) or of loans for some types of building (e.g., dormitories) influences governing boards and presidents to develop their institutions in some ways rather than in others.

Legislative Pressures

In some instances appropriations from state governments have been used to exercise limiting or interfering authority by denying funds for research or teaching in fields that legislators did not favor, or by making available funds for research in fields (e.g., poultry in Louisiana) that they did favor. In other instances, state legislatures have threatened both public and private institutions with discriminatory or regulatory legislation and have subjected them to questioning by investigating committees. Loyalty oath legislation, and threats of such, have constituted a form of such pressure. In still other instances, the pressures of legislators have resulted in the establishment of teaching and research in labor relations, or in the prevention of racial, religious, or ethnic discrimination in admissions.

The pressures of state legislatures, in summary, may constitute healthy influences tending to keep institutions attuned to the needs of the society they serve, or they may constitute the abridgment of academic freedom by denying support for teaching or research that legislators do not understand. They may constitute petty or even unethical interference in management, e.g., direction that the football schedule be altered, or insistence that supplies be bought through a favored supplier.

Administrative Controls

More often, and less apparently, are the decisions of administrators influenced by irksome and usually unnecessary administrative controls exercised by state governments. These controls may take the form of administrative limitations set by state budget officers, requirements that supplies and equipment be obtained through a centralized state purchasing office or that buildings be planned or approved by a statewide building division, or application of civil service provisions to nonacademic, and sometimes academic, personnel.[19]

Such encroachments by state agencies have given rise, in recent years, to increasing concern. A former president of West Virginia University, for example, has complained that his institution "may not belong to any organization without prior approval of the Board of Public Works" and that his administration suffered from the "capriciousness of the State Auditor."[20] His experience, more courageously and forthrightly stated than the experience of many others, is confirmed by the presidents of a number of other state universities.

Tax Exemptions

Threats to the tax exemption status of private colleges have been pointed to by some as an additional mechanism through which government might force conformity of these institutions. The legislature of Massachusetts, for example, a few years ago considered legislation to withdraw tax exemption status from colleges which did not admit a higher proportion of residents. The

[19] For a full, well-documented description and discussion of the nature and effect of such controls see Moos and Rourke, *op. cit.*, and *The Efficiency of Freedom*, the report of the Committee on Government and Higher Education, Johns Hopkins Press, Baltimore, 1959.

[20] "West Virginia University, 1946–58, Report of President Irvin Stewart," *West Virginia University Bulletin*, June, 1958. Similar situations exist in other states. Personnel of higher institutions in Oregon must submit travel requests, purchases, and other proposed expenditures to offices in the state capitol for approval despite budgetary appropriations.

legislation was not passed. Yet the proposal that it be enacted to force the adoption of a course which the institutions had not deemed wise to follow gave rise to fears that this mechanism might be used to force conformity with other dictates.

The administrators of state institutions, like the administrators of other public functions, e.g., the construction of highways, obviously must be sensitive to (as well as lead) legislative and public opinion. Yet the history of education in this country has demonstrated that if universities are to advance new ideas, to reinterpret old ideas, and objectively to challenge established opinions and practices, they must be granted a broad measure of independence. The accumulation of encroachments in the name of "coordination," "administrative efficiency," or "economy" assumes especial importance when the numbers being educated and the role being performed by the state universities are growing much larger than those of the private institutions which enjoy greater independence.

ACCREDITATION AND DECISION MAKING

The external control of the academic standards of American colleges and universities differs markedly from that which obtains in other countries. *Accreditation,* as the process of control is termed in this country, is in contrast predominantly a nongovernmental process. It is carried out by six regional associations of colleges and universities, by thirty national professional organizations,[21] and by one state agency—the State University of New York. The regional associations (e.g., North Central Association of Sec-

[21] The National Commission on Accrediting has identified four categories of accrediting associations: quasi-accrediting organizations such as Phi Beta Kappa and the American Association of University Women; the six regional accrediting associations; the professional and divisional associations such as the American Psychological Association and the American Association of Junior Colleges; and the professional associations which have a legislative foundation for their requirements, such as the American Bar Association and the American Medical Association. For full description of the organizations engaged in this activity see Lloyd E. Blauch (ed.), *Accreditation in Higher Education,* U.S. Office of Education, Washington, 1959.

ondary Schools and Colleges) are essentially groups of colleges and universities. The professional associations (e.g., American Chemical Society, Association of Collegiate Schools of Business, and American Bar Association) are associations of faculty members.

These accrediting associations represent their members but simultaneously perform a semipublic function. This function involves, in varying degrees between the individual associations, four principal purposes: (1) assurance of the maintenance of adequate admission requirements, (2) maintenance of minimum academic standards, (3) stimulation of institutional self-improvement, and (4) provision of a countervailing force against many external and internal pressures that would subvert the institution from its true goals.[22]

In performing their semipublic function these associations establish criteria by which to measure the capabilities of individual institutions. They apply these criteria on the basis of reports made by the institutions and by on-the-campus inspections of teams made up of individuals usually recruited from other institutions' faculties. They strive to have institutions conform with the established criteria and may imply, or threaten, nonaccreditation if they do not do so.

The influence of accrediting associations is often felt by college and university administrators more forcefully through the institution's own faculties. Departmental faculties naturally are concerned by the evaluation of their peers, e.g., a chemistry faculty is much concerned if a team from the American Chemical Society concludes that the department does not meet the criteria. They are naturally and legitimately concerned if graduate schools do not admit their students because deficiencies in the institution are reported by professional accrediting groups. Consequently faculty members tend to carry their views into the decision-making councils of the institution. They strive to obtain the approval and the resources that will enable them to meet the professional accrediting

[22] William K. Selden, *Accreditation, a Struggle over Standards in Higher Education,* a monograph prepared by the executive secretary of the National Commission on Accrediting, Harper & Brothers, New York, 1959, pp. 42–43.

standards in terms of staff, facilities, equipment, library facilities, and other matters.

They may strive to achieve their ends by presenting their arguments directly to the institution's administrators. Or they may more subtly motivate alumni who are members of the same profession, e.g., doctors, nurses, or chemists, to espouse their cause. Sometimes alumnae who feel a limitation on their social standing when the American Association of University Women does not recognize their alma mater may agitate for whatever changes are required to gain approval.

The influence of these associations has been debated (and oftentimes resented) by college and university presidents for several decades.[23] Two dangers are stressed: segmentation and the reinforcement of standpattism. First, most professional accrediting associations tend "to view a university as an arrangement for expediting administration of autonomous faculties" rather than "as an institution which has purposes and values greater than its parts."[24] Thus, presidents find their institutions subject to pressures from a number of agencies seeking conformance to externally determined standards set without regard to the other functions of colleges and universities.

Second, professional and regional accrediting associations tend to discourage change in curricula, teaching method, or practice. Departmental realignment or collaboration may be questioned. Experimentation that veers from conventional academic organization and practice may not pass muster when measured against standards reflecting the past.

Professional associations and accrediting agencies, however, do exercise a positive influence which may assist the president looking for support. A principal example has been the effort of the American Medical Association to raise standards for medical education

[23] Samuel P. Capen (the late chancellor of the University of Buffalo) described the accreditation system as "competitive blackmail . . . of the boards and administrative officers." See *The Management of Universities*, Henry Stewart Inc., Buffalo, 1953, pp. 270ff.

[24] Fred O. Pinkham, "The Accreditation Problem," *The Annals*, American Academy of Political and Social Science, 301:65–74, September, 1955, p. 73.

(some university presidents have feared that standards were to be raised even at the cost of bankruptcy for the institution!). Currently both the chemical and the engineering societies maintain a continuing interest in the improvement of college teaching. While, on the one hand, departmental chairmen may submit demands for increased facilities and staffs on the basis of professional criteria, presidents on occasion instigate investigations by professional associations to bring to light departmental insufficiencies.

The problem this poses for decision making is basic to all external pressures: how to maintain institutional integrity, yet remain responsive to the needs of society when those needs are accurately expressed by the accrediting and professional associations.

THE INFLUENCE OF DONORS

Higher education in this country, especially the private colleges and universities, has long been indebted to generous donors for the funds that have made their operation and growth possible. These donors include religious bodies, individuals of means, foundations, alumni (whose influence has been considered), and business enterprises. Many of the gifts of these donors, like the support of government and of contractors for research, have emphasized certain activities and tended to neglect others, e.g., athletics or the physical sciences rather than libraries or faculty salaries. And a few donors have used their gifts as the means to impose their beliefs upon instruction, curriculum, and research.

Since World War II, two developments tend to pose new questions about what influence donors will have over institutional policies. Corporate giving has grown from $30 million in 1936 to $314 million in 1954. Tax laws and economic growth have brought about the establishment of an increased number of foundations with vastly increased resources. As colleges and universities increasingly turn to these sources for imperative additions to their incomes,[25]

[25] One important consideration in an evaluation of private philanthropy is the high degree of concentration to the "prestige universities and colleges." Thus, in 1954, 18 institutions (only 1 per cent) received nearly 45 per cent of the total

presidents and administrators need to examine intelligently the kinds of influences—frequently more subtle than direct—which such support will bring.

Corporate support has taken three basic forms. One is the provision of funds for special projects, usually in the form of contractual research (as discussed above). A second is the allotment of funds for scholarships and fellowships and for the refund of tuition paid by employees. A third is gifts, distributed among different types of colleges and universities, although favoring private as against public institutions.

In accepting such support, institutions will likely be confronted with an indeterminate amount of indirect and direct influence. The scholarships donated by corporations and the research contracts and grants made will usually encourage and support applied rather than theoretical studies. Many business firms will not give to universities whose faculties are noted for criticism of the existing economic system, or which have been involved in controversial issues. Some business executives will endeavor to use the donations they make, in behalf of their corporate employers, to force presidents, deans, and faculties to accept their (the executives') uninformed views on education.

Increasingly, moreover, businessmen incline to examine the administrative efficiency of universities to which they make donations. "To court a share in the corporate funds currently being made available to universities," noted the recorder of a recent meeting at which corporate philanthropy was discussed, "institutions must muffle talk about budgetary deficits and be prepared to answer searching questions about the efficiency of their management and organization." [26]

---

endowment funds; 805 institutions (43 per cent) had no endowment income at all, although they enrolled one-quarter of the students. V. C. Blum, "Financing Higher Education," *Journal of Higher Education*, 29:309–316, June, 1958, p. 310.

[26] Wilson Compton, "Corporation Support," *The Annals*, American Academy of Political and Social Science, 301:140–147, September, 1955, p. 146. (In discussion following Mr. Compton's talk.)

Foundation Influence

Foundation influence upon colleges and universities, their administrators and their faculties, has been sufficient to provoke two congressional investigations. Both politically inspired investigations sought unsuccessfully to reveal some undesirable motivation for the grants and actions of major foundations. But foundations do influence substantially the governance, particularly of the best, of this country's colleges and universities. And the presidents, many deans, and outstanding scholars count it an asset to know and be favorably known by officials of the major foundations.[27]

Foundations influence internal decision making by granting the substantial sums (more than $250 million) that they parcel out annually. By making grants for research in some fields, for some experiments in educational method, and for some developments rather than others, they materially influence the course that institutions, scholars, and teachers follow. To some extent they influence applicants to seek aid for projects tailored to what the applicants think are the foundation's interests, rather than the applicant's own interests or those of the institution with which he is affiliated.

Jacques Barzun, in delightful prose, has lambasted foundations.[28] He complains of their methods of selecting those to whom they provide aid, of their encouragement of conferences ("a substitute for work"), and of their emphasis on carefully "projected" objec-

---

[27] The term *major foundations* customarily means general welfare foundations with resources of $10 million or more. Among these the best known are the Ford, Rockefeller, Carnegie, Sloan, Mellon, Kellogg, Commonwealth, Guggenheim, Hayden, and Lilly foundations. For a good summary discussion of the influence of such foundations see W. Homer Turner, "The Prospects for Private Sector Support of Higher Education," chap. 10 in *Financing Higher Education: 1960–1970*, pp. 234–238.

[28] *The House of Intellect*, Harper & Brothers, New York, 1959, chap. 7, "The Folklore of Philanthropy," pp. 175–198. For a contrasting viewpoint on the role of the foundation in promoting educational "innovation" see David Riesman, "Planning in Higher Education: Patterns and Problems," *Human Organization*, 18(1):15–16, spring, 1959.

tives rather than on the "intellectual ambition and power" of the individual. One wonders, as one reads, whether Barzun writes with his tongue in his cheek. For by and large the record of the foundations for seeking out individuals with especially able and creative minds (be they researchers, scholars, or administrators) and supporting them in the work they want to do is unimpeachable.

Many foundations avowedly seek to aid certain kinds of educational improvement and reform. The Center for the Study of Liberal Education of the Ford Foundation, for example, has sought to increase the emphasis that evening colleges give to the liberal or general studies. Similarly, the Fund for Adult Education, in 1951, launched "a nation-wide effort to help expand educational opportunity for leaders." These, and other foundations in other fields, by the very announcement of their willingness to provide support for certain kinds of work induce presidents, deans, and scholars to undertake projects they might not otherwise have conceived.

Perhaps the greatest influence of foundations is through the advice provided by their officials. These men travel broadly. They familiarize themselves with most of the good work being done throughout the country in the field which interests them.[29] They are consulted by scholars who seek the benefit of their comprehensive knowledge of the work being done by other scholars. They aid scholars also by identifying problems of current significance and bringing preeminent administrators or scholars together to discuss and plan attacks upon them. And finally their counsel is sought by deans looking for new faculty members, by presidents seeking new deans, and often by trustees seeking presidents for their institutions.

The influence of foundations, in contrast with that of alumni, contractors for research, and governmental agencies, is more passively exercised. They seek the ablest administrators and scholars, but their aid is more often sought than proffered. Their influence

[29] For a thoughtful, humble, and well-written description of the work of a foundation see the statement of John W. Gardner, president, in the 1955 Annual Report of the Carnegie Corporation.

is incalculable, however, in that they are often providing the "venture capital" for educational advance, for research in little-explored fields, for launching unprecedented courses or seminars, for experimentation with new administrative arrangements. In deciding what individuals and institutions merit support, and in exercising the prescience and prevision required to single out those studies, those experiments in educational program, teaching method, and administrative arrangement that promise to contribute most to educational advance, foundation officials accept a large responsibility and exercise great influence. And the record of foundation action demonstrates that this influence has been exercised by distinguished and conscientious trustees and outstandingly capable and socially responsible officials.[30]

AGGREGATE EFFECT OF EXTERNAL GROUPS

The identification on preceding pages of some groups that influence the decisions of presidents, deans, faculties, and trustees, and the summary consideration of the nature and extent of their influence, does not picture all groups that exercise some influence, e.g., churches and religious orders, nor presume to analyze definitively the nature and extent of pressure exercised. The purpose here has been to describe this aspect of the environment within which institutional governance is carried on. This description suggests simultaneously how little ordered analysis has been made of the effect of external groups upon the governance of colleges and universities. At least the following lines of analysis deserve the attention of students of university administration.

1. Much has been written and said about the financial importance of alumni, government, contractors, and donors and of the distortionary influence they (and accrediting agencies) exercise. Little has been written about their influence in communicating the changing needs of the society to our colleges and universities and in prodding them to adapt programs to evolving needs. The

[30] Turner, op. cit., p. 236.

study of their influence on significant change in courses and curricula deserves analysis.

2. No studies are available to show where in the institution the impact of each group is felt. That alumni press for better football teams through the coach or graduate director of athletics may be clear. But how does the government research contract, the business firm's appeal for courses to train its employees, or the pressure of the accrediting association for the expansion of faculty or library facilities come to the president? Such proposals are often developed with the collaboration, or stimulation, of members of the faculty. The difficulties of coping with resulting proposals, and of harnessing the support available from these groups for the institution's good, may be largely attributable to the manner in which these forces "penetrate" the institution.

3. Studies of university administration to date have devoted little attention to the structural arrangements that best provide for the orderly handling of relationships with each of these several forces. There are analyses of the emerging role of the "vice president for development" and of his relationship to the alumni secretary, the alumni, foundations, and donors. There is some material describing alternative arrangements for coordinating research and relationships with contractors. There are analyses of the dean of students' responsibility for relationships with parents. What is needed next is a consideration of the totality of an institution's external relationships and the assignment of organizational responsibilities for their handling.

In summary, the problem of how the pressures of external groups can be handled that their impact on decision making will be "right" is an infinitely complex one. Some of the pressures put forward are good, some bad. How are they to be sorted out, and according to what principles that apply particularly to higher education? By whom are they to be handled—trustees, president, faculty, or groups within the society who support these institutions? Light shed on these questions will be infinitely valuable.

Chapter 8

INSTITUTIONAL CHARACTER
AND LEADERSHIP: THEIR EFFECT
ON GOVERNANCE

PURSUIT OF PURPOSE

WHAT SUSTAINS a college or university in the persistent pursuit of considered, worthy purposes? In the face of the rivalries and conflicts that prevail among schools and departments, of the frictions between faculty and administration, and of the pressures manifested from without by alumni, contractors, constituencies served, professional associations, and financial supporters, what forces ensure the integrity of a college or university?

By integrity is meant more than administrative efficiency and economy of operation—much more. What is meant is the consistent pursuit of agreed-upon purposes, the maintenance of high standards of performance in achieving these purposes, and the loyal concentration of a high proportion of the energies and interests of members of the enterprise upon these purposes. Integrity is only secondarily a consequence of the logic of organization or the efficiency of forms and procedures. It is predominantly the consequence of whatever forces focus the policies, decisions, and loyalties of all members of the enterprise on common objectives and values.

Organizations—be they business firms, governmental agencies, or universities—arrive at many decisions that represent an attainable consensus among individuals participating in the decision making.[1] And thus it must be. For decisions are, in considerable part, the result of conflict between tradition and the demand for change. They are the product of friction between contrasting philosophies. They are distilled from the currents and countercurrents that stem from the ambitions, anxieties, resistances, strivings, and understandings of individuals within and groups from without the institution.[2]

In the business firm the dominating objective of profit helps to resolve differences that stem from such conflict, friction, ambitions, and limited understandings. In the government agency the exposure to public review similarly serves to ensure the resolution of differences in the organization's interest. In both forms of organization (to lesser degree in the latter than in the former) there is a final, central source of decision-making authority: the chief executive.

In the law firm, in the hospital, or in the firm of architects or of consultants, professional standards aid in resolving the conflict of views and ambitions that arise in decision making. Each of these enterprises is dependent upon the interests and talents of its staff. In each, staff members customarily insist upon substantial freedom from direction in the methods by which they carry on their work, the clients or patients that they will choose to serve, the problems on which the individual will work, and the conclusions that they reach. While motivated by profit in varying degrees, the lawyers, doctors, nurses, architects, and consultants are guided in their decisions by professional standards which ensure that a lawyer will

[1] See, for the elaboration of a similar view, Chester I. Barnard, *The Functions of the Executive*, Harvard University Press, Cambridge, Mass., 1950, chap. 13, "The Environment of Decision"; Herbert A. Simon, *Administrative Behavior*, The Macmillan Company, New York, 1947, chaps. 1, 3, and 4; and Marshall Dimock, *A Philosophy of Administration*, Harper & Brothers, New York, 1958, chap. 15, "Decisions."

[2] William J. Gore and Fred S. Silander, "A Bibliographical Essay on Decision Making," *Administrative Science Quarterly*, June, 1959, p. 99.

not decide questions as would a "shyster" and that an architect will not make decisions as would a "jerry-builder."

In the university, the chief executive usually does not have so great and final an authority for decision making as does his counterpart in business or government. Nor are the professional standards that guide the faculty member in making decisions on educational programing so clear and generally influential as are those of the doctor, the lawyer, and some other professional men. And, of course, the prospect neither of profit nor (to so great a degree as in the governmental agency) of public review lends assurance that the consensus that is arrived at by faculty, deans, president, and trustees will be in the institution's interest.

What, then, can be relied upon to assure that decisions within a college or university will constitute the persistent pursuit of considered worthy purposes? What interrelates and gives progressive direction to the succession of decisions that constitute the functioning of each such organization? Two forces that exist, but often play a lesser part, in other forms of enterprise make for integrity in the decision making of colleges and universities. The college and the university, in substantial measure, are dependent upon (1) the existence of an institutional character and (2) the availability of creative leadership capable of persistently fashioning an organism that accepts new tasks and purposes consistent with its character.

INTERNAL CHALLENGES TO PURPOSE

The burden imposed upon these two forces—character and leadership—is large. It is made large by the extent to which decision making is dispersed within the college or university, and by the prevalence of significant issues that give rise to conflict, friction, and competition. Here it is proposed, before defining the nature and describing the role of institutional character and of creative leadership, to picture the nature of issues underlying decision making.

The Issue of Purpose

A prime source of conflict within colleges and universities has to do with the basic purpose or purposes of higher education: to provide a broadly based cultural education, or to equip students to earn a living? Simultaneously there is often conflict about the relative responsibility of the institution for providing community services, for research, and for teaching. The demands of the community for services—lectures, surveys, committee participation, and the like—and the demands of government and other contractors for research give rise to such conflict. Some administrators and some teachers tend to fulfill such demands even to the neglect of teaching; other administrators and many teachers tend to view them as interference with the purpose—teaching.

Such differences within, among faculty members and administrators and trustees, are echoed and reinforced from without. Parents often manifest a pragmatic desire to have their children equipped to earn a living; they tend to emphasize vocationally oriented courses that have, in their eyes, a practical utility. Similarly, the business or governmental agency that looks to the university to aid in training its employees or in research to improve its products will often emphasize one purpose at the expense of others. For example, decisions to accept grants for research from the government agency responsible for the cultivation of our forests (the U.S. Forest Service), or from the agency responsible for the exploration of space (the National Aeronautics and Space Administration), or from the agency responsible for the discovery of the causes and cures for disease (the U.S. Public Health Service) are decisions that may emphasize research at the expense of teaching or may foster some departments at the expense of others.

The Issue of Method

Perhaps even more vigorous conflict arises within colleges and universities over the method to be followed in achieving their educational purpose. Two common manifestations of such conflict are the differences that arise (1) over the issue of general education versus emphasis on the disciplines, and (2) over the responsibility of the institution to provide, in addition to instruction, a variety of athletic, recreational, personal counseling, vocational guidance, and related services.[3] Again the differences that arise within the institution are echoed and reinforced by parents and alumni from without.

The Issue of Size vs. Standards

The resignation of five professors at Lamar State College of Technology in Beaumont, Texas,[4] illustrates another source of conflict underlying academic decision making. Lamar College, a young, publicly supported university, within recent years has expanded rapidly in physical facilities and in enrollment. The five professors, it was reported, resigned because they believed they had been asked to lower standards of instruction in their classes to facilitate further growth in enrollment.

In their best form these issues involve the question of "who is worth education." Often the issue arises in terms of "size versus standards." For such prestige institutions as Cornell, Princeton, Stanford, and Wesleyan the issue usually takes the form of these questions: Must we enroll more students and risk lowering academic standards? Or shall we raise admission standards and keep enrollment at present levels? For other institutions, e.g., Beloit College, the issue takes the urgent form this question implies: Can we balance our budget at any higher level of admission standards?

Administrative officers plagued with rising costs and the need for new facilities often are inclined to seek the increased revenues that increased enrollment would bring. The academics, attaching greater importance to standards of admission and to subsequent academic performance, tend to oppose growth that might relieve financial pressures.

The Issue of the Whole or the Parts

A fourth area of differences among the participants in governance arises out of the contrasting breadths of concern of adminis-

[3] *Ibid.*, pp. 120–134, 152–160.
[4] The *Beaumont Enterprise*, June 4, 1959.

trators and of academics. Deans and department heads tend to be concerned, primarily or solely, with the furtherance of their respective schools or departments. The trustees, and particularly the president, must differ with them on many issues, for it is their responsibility to balance the interests of every part to achieve the greatest good for the whole.

The president (and subsequently the trustees) are sometimes confronted with similar differences by the efforts of accrediting associations to raise standards of instruction, at least as they see such standards. The professional accrediting association sometimes illustrates that one group's standards can be another group's nonsense. In striving to advance the profession that it represents—chemistry, education, law, or medicine—it may dictate that an institution expand its faculty in the particular field, that salaries be increased, or that standards of admission be raised in order to limit the number of new entrants into the profession.

Kenneth Boulding has argued that "every professional society is a conspiracy against the public." [5] Perhaps he overstates the point, but this much is clear: The influence exercised by the professional accrediting association is not founded on a balanced concern with each of the various departments and schools which make up the university, and which must receive the balanced consideration of those responsible for internal decision making if the institution is to serve its students, and the society, well.

The Issue of Information

Closely related to the issue of the whole or the parts is the issue of information. In other forms of enterprise, the lack of common information gives rise to differences and conflict between division and department heads within, and with suppliers, customers, bankers, or legislators without. In the college or university the high order of specialization among and within departments and schools, the lack of a clearly defined, single purpose, the frequent lack of

[5] "An Economist's View of the Manpower Concept," *Proceedings of a Conference on the Utilization of Scientific and Professional Manpower,* National Manpower Council, Columbia University Press, New York, 1954, pp. 11–25.

means or effort to communicate information about educational programing (e.g., the modification of a course) among participants, and the general dispersal of authority for decision making tend to lend importance to this issue.

Moreover, the issue assumes a unique form through the participation of alumni in institutional decision making. It is often the alumni—men and women associated by a common and abiding interest in their alma mater—who form the external force that manifests the greatest lack of information about the institution's accepted purposes. The college or university president plagued with a critical need for resources with which to raise salaries, or with which to construct a new library or laboratory, is understandably disheartened by the alumni's greater interest in subsidizing the football team or in building a new field house.

The fault—the alumni's lack of appreciation of the greater urgency of needs that affect the central purpose of the institution's being—may be his (the president's) own. But that, for the moment, is beside the point. Decision making in many (especially the private) institutions of higher education is increasingly influenced by the willingness of alumni to provide financial support. And that influence often does not contribute to the basic objectives of the institution.

No one of the foregoing issues is peculiar to the academic enterprise; each can be detected as a source of conflict, differences, friction, and competition that plague decision making, at times, in business, governmental, religious, military, and other forms of enterprise. Yet, it is believed, these issues arise more frequently and engender more vigorous conflict in the college or university than in other forms of enterprise. Thus they make more difficult the task of assuring that decisions will constitute the persistent pursuit of considered, worthy purposes.

CHARACTERISTICS COMPLICATING DECISION MAKING

This task is made still the more difficult by three characteristics of the academic enterprise. Again, these characteristics are not peculiar to the college or university. They are more common among these enterprises, however, and seemingly more consistently influential.

Resistance to Change in Academic Situations

Individuals and groups within most enterprises tend to resist adaptation to new conditions, and hence to preserve existing practices. Human beings tend to find a sense of security in an accustomed system and to view changes as threats to power and status. In the college or university this general human tendency is accentuated by many aspects of the academic situation.

Faculty members concerned with the liberal arts or with the professions tend to suspect change suggested by groups that are external either to the institution or to their discipline or profession. Appeals to change courses or curricula to meet developments within the society are often viewed by academics as demands that the faculty disloyally sacrifice old and venerated values.[6] Until and unless, as David Riesman has pointed out, other prestige institutions make such changes in their educational programs they are usually stoutly resisted.[7]

Faculty members, concentrating on their respective disciplines, seldom concern themselves with broader educational problems. Yet they tend to resist changes in educational program or method. Consider, for example, the general reaction to proposals for the introduction of larger classes or for improved methods of scholastic achievement testing or occupational guidance.

Finally, faculty members usually lack interest in administrative operations. They tend to be insensitive to the need for organizational or procedural change, e.g., the introduction of new processes to govern the hiring and compensation of secretaries or the procurement of supplies. Yet it is such businesslike methods that businesslike trustees want.

[6] Charles Frankel (ed.), *Issues in University Education*, Harper & Brothers, New York, 1959, especially chaps. 2 and 3, pp. 24–62.

[7] *Constraint and Variety in Education*, University of Nebraska Press, Lincoln, Nebr., 1956, chap. 1.

The Impact of Structure of Academic Organization on Adjustment

The dispersion of decision-making authority with respect to educational program or faculty selection among the participants within the institution, the autonomy of departments, the freedom of the individual from hierarchical direction, the commitment of scholars to their disciplines and professions (more than to their employers)—these and other characteristics of the structure of academic organization constitute a set of antibodies that protect the academic program and faculty against educational evolution.

The president, confronted with the demands of alumni or legislatures, must recognize these internal forces and achieve such adjustment as he and his fellow academic officers are convinced are desirable, despite or consistent with these structural characteristics. The president is indeed in between, but this may be, for the educator skilled in persuasion and endowed with powers of leadership, an opportunity rather than a curse.

To the extent that such structural characteristics discourage creative adaptation to a changing society, they undermine institutional effectiveness. On the other hand, they may ensure consistent allegiance to the distinctive purpose of the particular institution. The new ideas, the new insights, and the expanded understanding of an evolving society that come from without can contribute to a dynamic and creative educational program. If the dispersed and relatively autonomous individuals that constitute the structure of an academic institution can be mobilized by president, by dean, by department head, or by faculty leaders in an open-minded effort to weigh these ideas, insights, and suggestions and to assimilate those which have permanent value in educational programs and to reject those which are of transitory significance, then educational progress will result.

The Effect of External-Internal Allegiances on Governance

The specialized departments and professional schools tend to seek the support of, or to voice internally the views of, their allied professional associations, e.g., the American Chemical Society. Administrators of the evening divisions are often supported by, or represent internally, local employers. The dean of the school of education and his faculty will likely be closely associated with the state educational association. The dean of agriculture will similarly have the backing of a strong agricultural constituency and will voice the views of that constituency in internal decision-making councils. Faculty members are often allied in thought with agencies that sponsor research, and especially with the professional society to which most belong. The football coach will likely have a well-mobilized body of alumni and local businessmen to back his appeals for financial support, and sometimes for liberalized academic standards. And trustees will normally reflect views similar to those of alumni, donors, legislators, and parents.

For the president and his academic and administrative officers these external-internal allegiances limit, or make difficult, the influencing of institutional decisions. Yet simultaneously they engender the conflict, differences, and competition that necessitate a guiding influence if the succession of institutional decisions is to reflect an institutional integrity.

INSTITUTIONAL CHARACTER—A GUIDING FORCE

The very nature and structure of a college or university, in short, ensure that decision making will be underlain with a greater measure of healthy, vigorous differences, conflict, friction, and competition. They reemphasize the question: What interrelates and gives progressive direction to the succession of decisions by individual teachers, faculty groups (committees or departments), directors of admission, deans of students, financial officers, or others that constitute the governance of a college or university? In short, what sustains the integrity of the institution?

Of late, perceptive observers of the functioning of business enterprises have pointed out that decision making is guided in considerable part by an influential force beyond (or in addition to) the stated goals, prospect of profit, or authority of the chief executive.

Adolf Berle has eloquently pictured how a variety of decisions, e.g., the disenfranchisement of a dealer by an automobile manufacturer, are guided by what he terms "the conscience of the corporation." [8] J. Douglas Brown, dean of faculties at Princeton University and an authority in the field of industrial relations, has indicated how the "personality" of the corporate enterprise influences the relations between the enterprise and its employees.[9] Robert B. Buchele has similarly written of "the characters of companies" and how they dress, as well as of such more substantial matters as the extent of delegation of authority and the quality and amount of training provided for employees.[10] And Pierre Martineau, director of research and marketing for the *Chicago Tribune*, has written stimulatingly of the "personality" of the department store, of the chain grocery store, of the automobile dealer, of the gasoline distributor, and of airlines.[11]

These authors have used, but have not precisely defined, the "character" of an enterprise. This lack is supplied by two of the growing number of sociologists concerning themselves with problems of organization. Talcott Parsons has pointed out that organizations can be (and usually are) described and organized in terms of "groups" and "roles," i.e., of what subdivisions the organization is made up and the function of each. Then, he adds, they can be described and analyzed from a "cultural-institutional" point of view, i.e., the values of the organization and how these are reflected in its structure and functioning—in short, in terms of its character.[12]

[8] *The 20th Century Capitalist Revolution,* Harcourt, Brace and Company, Inc., New York, 1954, chap. 3, "The Conscience of the King and of the Corporation."

[9] *High Talent Manpower for Science and Industry,* Research Report Series, no. 95, Industrial Relations Section, Princeton University, Princeton, N.J., 1957.

[10] "Company Character and the Effectiveness of Personnel Management," *Personnel,* January, 1955, pp. 289–302.

[11] "The Personality of the Retail Store," *Harvard Business Review,* January-February, 1958.

[12] "Sociological Approach to the Theory of Organizations—I," *Administrative Science Quarterly,* June, 1956, p. 67.

Philip Selznick helpfully expands on this analysis. He defines *character* as "the distinctive competence or inadequacy that an organization has acquired." This character, he asserts, will be disclosed by examining "the commitments that have been accepted in the course of adaptation to internal and external pressures." He exemplifies his concept by picturing the character of the Agricultural Extension Service in terms of these related commitments: (1) the involvement of the county agricultural agent in "courthouse" politics; (2) the intimate relation between the Extension Service and the American Farm Bureau Federation; (3) a tendency of the extension agents to deal with the relatively more prosperous elements of the local farm population and to reflect certain dominant attitudes, such as those toward farm tenancy; (4) a shift in the role of the Extension Service from a primary educational emphasis to the acceptance of responsibility for "action programs." These and related commitments determine the competence or inadequacy of the Extension Service for particular assignments and thus form, he contends, "its relevant character." Finally, he adds, the organizational character will be reflected by the social composition of the membership of the enterprise; "organizations that are self-conscious about their characters—an officers' corps, an elite school, etc.—normally attempt to control composition by being selective, so that only persons having appropriate social origins are accepted." [13]

THE CHARACTER OF THE UNIVERSITY

That colleges and universities have characters is, as was stated by Dean De Vane of Yale, apparent to anyone "who travels from, let us say, Harvard to Columbia, from Yale to Michigan, to say nothing of moving from Tulane to California." [14] It is equally apparent to anyone who observes, as the author has, the functioning of the colleges and universities studied as a basis for understanding

[13] *Leadership in Administration,* Row, Peterson & Company, Evanston, Ill., 1959, pp. 42–46.
[14] William C. De Vane, *The American University in the Twentieth Century,* Louisiana State University Press, Baton Rouge, La., 1957, p. 14.

governance. There are clearly distinguishable differences in the "commitments" and in the "social composition" of faculty membership that form the characters of Stanford and George Washington, of Princeton and Georgetown, of Wesleyan and Toledo, of Minnesota and Virginia, of Beloit and Goucher, and even of Denison and Carleton.

Contrast, for example, Stanford and George Washington universities. Their commitments, in terms of kind of educational program and the constituency each chooses to serve, and in terms of the origins and make-up of faculty, vary markedly. Stanford has committed itself to the liberal arts with especial emphasis on graduate training, particularly in the sciences. Its faculty is respected for a high level of academic excellence, is recruited from the graduate schools that lead in each discipline or from other prestige institutions, and is generally engaged in significant research. George Washington offers a greater array of courses in a variety of fields; there is less apparent emphasis on the liberal arts, on graduate training, or on research; there is an obvious tendency to offer courses designed to serve the vocational interests of individuals employed by the District of Columbia's major employer, the Federal government. Its full-time members are less often recruited from the prestige institutions, and a smaller proportion are recognized for their writings on research.

Stanford limits its enrollment to approximately 6,000 full-time resident students; George Washington has a total student body of 15,000; it has few resident students and many part-time students. At Stanford, of every four applicants for enrollment three are turned down; at George Washington few among those who apply for admission are not accepted; the institution's avowed function is to serve the community in which it is located, which is interpreted to mean acceptance of the bulk of all students above a workable admission level.

Both institutions are privately supported. Both are dependent, in significant part, on the largess of their respective alumni, of donors, and of foundations. Stanford has been able to build these relationships in a fashion more productive than most American universities. It receives substantial gifts annually from its alumni, and substantial donations. George Washington receives modest income from its alumni, and less from foundations and donors.

Stanford faculty members are organized in strong and somewhat insulated departments, yet the whole faculty resides within a smaller community, Palo Alto, which fosters some intercourse. The George Washington faculty is, in contrast, a more dispersed group. Its members reside throughout a large metropolitan area. Few individual members know many of their colleagues on the faculty. A large part of the faculty is made up of part-time teachers who have limited ties to the institution. A result, perhaps, of these factors is that the Stanford faculty has a substantially greater part in the making of decisions on educational program and faculty selection than does the George Washington faculty. At George Washington departments have less authority for governance; decision-making responsibility is concentrated to a greater degree in the president and his immediate staff.

George Washington is committed to serve the community in which it is located. Its educational program is molded by this influence; its faculty gives a substantial portion of its time to meeting the requests of civic institutions for speeches and a variety of services. Stanford looks to a larger community; it regards itself as the preeminent private institution in the West; it seeks a national student body.

The sum total of the factors mentioned is the institutionalized value system of trustees, president, deans, department heads, and faculty. It is the complex of "commitments that have been accepted in the course of adaptation to internal and external pressures." [15] None of the comparisons made between these institutions is intended to imply that the commitments of one are better than those of the other; in each instance they have been adaptations to the ecology in which the institution has found itself. The sum total is what we call *institutional character*.

[15] Selznick, *op. cit.*, p. 42.

A MAJOR INFLUENCE

Many readers may consider this concept of character as vague and inexact. It is. Yet in an organization in which no guides for day-to-day decision making are provided by precisely planned objectives,[16] by tangible profit measures of achievement, or by a chief executive possessing substantial, final authority, this intangible, unformulated, and even unrecognized force is a major influence on governance.

The character of the institution sets the boundaries within which participants may define or redefine its reason for existence and the activities to be performed. It is this character which establishes the guidelines for rational discussion by individuals and groups holding widely divergent values. It is this character which gives faculty members and students alike a sense of pride, or leaves them untouched as time-serving teachers and attendants. It is this character which influences the succession of critical decisions about educational program, admission standards, selection of faculty, and related matters that make the institution what it is.[17]

THE STILL GREATER INFLUENCE OF LEADERSHIP

The influence of institutional character is clear, is tangible, and is undeniable. Yet if one thing is certain in the administration of human enterprises, particularly those of large size, it is that, where

[16] The college or university often states such objectives as "to develop the well-rounded man," "to develop the individual," "to give students the greatest possible opportunity to develop their individual capabilities," etc. For an amusing and stimulating discussion relevant to the general and intangible objectives of institutions of higher education, see William C. Fels, "Modern College Usage," *Columbia University Forum,* spring, 1959.

[17] Huston Smith writes: "Any college worthy of the name will have a spiritual life of its own which makes of it more than an assemblage of teachers, students and buildings. At best it will have an atmosphere which is felt to be different from other environments the moment one steps into it and which acts as a powerful developing force upon all who live within it." *The Purposes of Higher Education,* Harper & Brothers, New York, 1955, p. 189.

no individual or group of individuals gives continual and progressive direction to the succession of decisions that constitute governance, its character changes and the institution retrogresses.[18] Challenged by the necessity of continually adapting its program to keep pace with society's needs, and handicapped by the widest dispersal of decision-making authority found in any form of human enterprise, the college or university is persistently threatened by the consequences of such lack of direction. That universities have lasted for eight centuries, have grown and are growing, and have exercised a substantial influence over the civilization that obtains wherever they are makes manifest that (with many exceptions) these institutions have possessed the leadership that was required.

In more authoritarian forms of enterprise—the business firm, the governmental agency, and particularly the military unit—such leadership is usually found in the person of the chief executive. Yet in such enterprises there are notable exceptions; an outstanding editor on a newspaper, an especially competent general manager of a department store, a career civil servant working under a succession of political department heads, or the farseeing planning officer in a military unit may provide the influence that focuses the enterprise on considered goals, maintains institutional integrity, and minimizes internal conflict. In the college or university such leadership is often (and is more apparent when) provided by the president. But such leadership may and has been frequently provided by a trustee, by a dean, by members of the faculty, or by a donor.

The task of leadership in the college or university may be supported or challenged by institutional character. At Harvard the tasks of leadership in keeping this great university abreast of the demands of the American civilization are large, but they are made less difficult by the character of the institution that its current leaders inherited. At the University of Virginia, somewhat in contrast,

[18] Certainly the president who presided over George Washington for thirty years—a graduate of Stanford, and one who was invited to return to his alma mater as president—has had a substantial part in creating this institution's character. Would the character of Stanford have been markedly changed had he returned to his alma mater?

Colgate Darden's proposals for making the university more responsive to the needs of the state were challeneged repeatedly by the institution's character. This university was committed traditionally to educating the sons of "the better families in the South" and to maintaining an environment similar to that of "socially superior" residential colleges. Hence, it found difficulty in accepting efforts to increase the number of enrollees from the state's high schools, to construct a student union building (which was branded as a manifestation of "State U-ism"), or to permit the attendance of women.

The task of college and university leadership is that of utilizing human, financial, physical, and spiritual resources to fashion an educational institution that persistently accepts new methods and programs but insists exactingly upon enduring values. That task, especially in the university, is infinitely more difficult than the task of leadership in the more authoritarian, more monolithic business firm, governmental agency, or military unit.[19] The leader in the academic institution must bring about consensus among a much larger proportion of members of the enterprise. He must achieve consensus among individuals, within and without the institution, with widely varying values. He must obtain financial and physical aid from sources that little understand, or that oppose, the values he stands for. He must, at times, accept the influence of the alumni or the legislature, knowing that it may alter the institution's character—and find ways to persuade either of the greater desirability of the values he seeks. And all this he must achieve with less power to direct, less general acceptance of clearly stated goals, and less opportunity to relate tangible results to proposals than his analogue in other forms of enterprise.

[19] Relevant, whether or not one agrees with the conclusion, is the comment of Vice President Nixon on the difference between "table pounding" and strong leadership. "Harry Truman," said Nixon, "was somewhat of a table pounder. He got results that way. Mr. Eisenhower is a persuader. He's gotten results, too. The problem of leadership cannot be described in terms of rigid, black and white categories. A President's success is determined by his results rather than how he did it." *Time*, Jan. 25, 1960.

MAJOR AREAS FOR EXPLORATION

The achievement of a better understanding of the governance of colleges and universities requires the study of each of the questions on organizational structure, on the distribution of responsibilities among participants, and on the mechanistic functioning of institutions that have been suggested in previous chapters. In addition, there is urgent need for the orderly, logical analysis of:

1. The characters of a number of contrasting—great and poor—colleges and universities

2. The nature of leadership (by presidents, but also by trustees, deans, faculty members, donors, and alumni) that has brought about greatness or has caused the decline of colleges and universities.

Through a succession of such analyses of particular colleges or universities, over a period of time, a more precise and fuller understanding of what institutional character is, how it is molded, and what influence it exercises can be learned. Simultaneously, through such analyses, more may be learned about how trustees, the president, deans or faculty officers, or faculty leaders can utilize or modify an institution's character to achieve ends they deem desirable.

These analyses alone will not reveal how the college or university as a social organism can be made more adequate to the demands of the decades ahead. Achievement of that end will require greater understanding of how each of the participants—trustees, president, deans, department heads, and faculty—can better make their contribution; of how the college or university differs as an administrative enterprise and how its processes need to be adapted to accommodate these differences; and of how the college or university can best "live with" the external groups who depend upon or support it. Achievement of that end will be the greater if the nature and influence of institutional character and the unique nature of institutional leadership can both be better understood.

Appendix A

CHARACTER OF THE
INSTITUTIONS OBSERVED

The selection of colleges and universities whose processes were to be observed at first hand and viewed through the opinions of trustees, administrators, and faculty was, in considerable part, opportunistic. A total of ten institutions were selected that were geographically accessible to the author's perambulations and headed by approachable individuals sympathetic with the author's curiosity about governance. Fortunately, they represent a workable sample of "prestige" private universities, of state universities, of denominational institutions, of urban universities, and of liberal arts colleges.

Here for the reader's guidance is a classified list of the institutions observed and some vital statistics [1] relative to each. After each of these institutions was visited (and in most instances revisited on two or more occasions), memoranda were written describing the governance as it had been observed through interviews and records. These memoranda were in each instance submitted for the review and criticism of officials of the institution and form the basis for many generalizations risked in this book.

[1] These vital statistics are founded on correspondence with officials of each of the selected institutions in December, 1959, and January, 1960. Because of differences in interpretation of the author's request and in the institutions' record-keeping systems, these data are not strictly comparable. They sufficiently acquaint the reader with the approximate size of each institution. No other use was made of these data.

Two private universities: Stanford [1959 enrollment, 8,784; faculty (including lecturers and instructors), 801; administrative staff, 955], a Western institution which consists of seven relatively separate schools: the College of Humanities and Sciences, a School of Mineral Sciences, a School of Education, a School of Engineering, a School of Law, a Medical School, and a Graduate School of Business; and *Princeton* (1959 enrollment, 3,780; faculty, 524), an integrated institution which does not include schools of law, medicine, or business, and within which schools of architecture, engineering, graduate studies, and public and international affairs are closely related with and oriented about the undergraduate liberal arts college.

Two urban universities: George Washington (1959 enrollment, 10,057; faculty, 1,578; administrative staff, 25), which is located in and serves a metropolitan area with the government of which it has no formal or financial ties; and the *University of Toledo* (1959 enrollment, 5,877; faculty, 303; administrative staff, 28), which serves a metropolitan area, the government of which gave birth to and continues to support and control the institution.

Two denominational universities: Georgetown (1959 enrollment, 6,150; faculty, 1,144; administrative staff, 307), an institution made up of seven separate schools operated by the Jesuit order; and *Denison* (1959 enrollment, 1,458; faculty, 113; administrative staff, 20), a smaller institution which is made up primarily of a liberal arts college and which throughout its history has been related to the Baptist Church.

Two state universities: Virginia (1959 enrollment, 4,786; faculty, 782; administrative staff, 36), an older state university which has persistently drawn a large proportion of out-of-state students and a relatively large proportion of its income from other than state appropriations; and *Minnesota* (1959 enrollment, 26,538; faculty, 2,074; administrative staff, 65), a large state university identified closely with the life of the state it serves and dependent in major part upon state appropriations.

Two liberal arts colleges: Goucher (1959 enrollment, 772; faculty, 76; administrative staff, 16), a small women's college with limited resources; and *Wesleyan* (1959 enrollment, 879; faculty, 132; administrative staff, 7), a college for men that emphasizes the liberal arts and has, in recent years, enjoyed relatively large resources with which to develop its educational program.

In addition to the observation of the governance of these institutions, this report presents the results of brief inquiries (made early in 1959) with trustees, officers, and faculty members in five Middle Western coeducational colleges of liberal arts: *Beloit* (1959 enrollment, 1,039; faculty, 83; administrative staff, 14); *Carleton* (1959 enrollment, 1,136; faculty, 108; administrative staff, 110[2]); *Grinnell* (1959 enrollment, 1,002; faculty, 75; administrative staff, 9); *Knox* (1959 enrollment, 869; faculty, 79; administrative staff, 56); and *Oberlin* (1959 enrollment, 2,359; faculty, 210; administrative staff, 41).

[2] This figure includes clerical and part-time employees.

Appendix B

COMMENTS ON SELECTED READINGS

Much has been written about colleges and universities, and the men and women who have made them run. Little has been written that measures up as an orderly and sophisticated analysis of why they are run the way they are run, and whether better ways can be found.

One student would seek material he regarded relevant to an examination of the processes of governance in these institutions in certain sources. Another student would delve into quite different ones. Thus, to enable the reader better to understand how this author arrived at many of the conclusions expressed in the body of this volume, this exhibit is presented. It enumerates many of the books, articles, and reports the author consulted and comments frankly on where he found material of value.

For purposes of this study this mass of literature [1] may be grouped in three major categories:

1. Works that depict the role of participants in the governing of an institution or institutions

2. Works that depict the administrative processes that obtain and

---

[1] The review of this literature has been materially facilitated by reference to Karl W. Bigelow's annotated bibliography, *Selected Books for the College and University Administrator*, Bureau of Publications, Teachers College, Columbia University, New York, 1958.

those that might obtain within an institution to facilitate the working together of faculty members, administrative employees, academic and administrative officers, and trustees

3. Works that depict the functioning of institutions as a whole as distinguished from the participants that make it up, or the processes used in its functioning

THE ROLE OF PARTICIPANTS

1. Trustees

Hubert Park Beck, in *The Men Who Control Our Universities*,[2] reported the results of a study of the membership of the governing boards of thirty leading American universities. His purpose, like that of Veblen [3] earlier, was to evaluate critically the membership of these boards in terms of their social origins, philosophical bents, and contributions to the effectiveness of the individual institution. Beck's book is the beacon of authors who are critical of today's boards of trustees. It criticizes the usual board's lack of representativeness and recommends a broader basis of functional representation on boards as a guarantor of society's stake in higher education.

In addition to Beck's book, the literature dealing with trustees and their functioning falls into three classes: (1) the comments of trustees themselves on their experiences; (2) works (or manuals) designed to tell trustees "how to do it," i.e., what their responsibilities are and how they should go about them; and (3) a few volumes that analyze the role of trustees in the field of education, as representatives of society and as administrators.

The first of these groups is typically reminiscent and affords little in the way of analysis on what the role of the trustees is or should be. Typical of the second group, i.e., the manuals, are works by Hughes,[4] Wicke,[5] and Rauh; [6] these afford useful aids to new

[2] King's Crown Press, New York, 1947.
[3] Thorstein Veblen, *Higher Learning in America,* The Viking Press, Inc., 1935.
[4] Raymond M. Hughes, *A Manual for Trustees of Colleges and Universities,* 3d ed., Iowa State College Press, Ames, Iowa, 1951.

trustees, but they do not attempt to appraise the role of the trustee.

Most important are those works which analyze critically the function the trustee should perform. Four works stand out in this field. The first is an address by Arthur S. Adams, "Relations Between Governing Boards and Administrative Officers." [7] The second is an address by Laird Bell, former chairman of the board of trustees of the University of Chicago; [8] this statement, with ruthless realism, appraises the role that trustees do and should perform for their institutions. The third is the significant "Paley report," *The Role of the Trustees of Columbia University.* The fourth is the provocative volume authored by Beardsley Ruml and Donald H. Morrison, *Memo to a College Trustee.*[9] Together these four statements point up well the problems of the role of trustees in the governance of colleges and universities. Wilmarth Lewis, a fellow of the Yale Corporation, speaking at Harvard in 1952, epitomized the problem these works dissect when he said, "The full duty of trustees is not evident even to trustees." [10]

Some additional material on the role of trustees is found in the writings of college presidents: Capen, Colwell, Day, Eliot, Hutchins, Griswold, McVey and Hughes, Wriston, and White. All are primarily historical or autobiographical, with an occasional flash to operations in action, and indicate the manner in which each president handled his relations with his trustees. These writings contribute generously to the body of information that gives insight into how our boards of trustees have become the kinds of boards that they are.

Yet there is little in these volumes to reflect a conscious evaluation of the role trustees in most institutions inherit comparable to

[5] Myron F. Wicke, *Handbook for Trustees,* Board of Education, The Methodist Church, Nashville, Tenn., 1957.

[6] Morton A. Rauh, *College and University Trusteeship,* The Antioch Press, Yellow Springs, Ohio, 1959.

[7] *Proceedings of the Association of Governing Boards of State Universities,* 1952, pp. 51–57.

[8] "From the Trustees' Corner," *Association of American Colleges Bulletin,* 42:353–361, October, 1956.

[9] McGraw-Hill Book Company, Inc., New York, 1959.

[10] "The Trustee and the University," *Harvard Alumni Bulletin,* July 2, 1952.

what Wilmarth Lewis did in defining the importance of the liaison functions of the trustees. Nor is much to be found in these volumes about (1) how the channels of communication to and from trustees can be improved, or (2) what part the trustees should have in the determination of educational policy. Donald C. Stone, formerly president of Springfield College and earlier an authority on problems of organization and management, has touched on the trustee role in his article on decision making in educational policy,[11] but even there it is covered only from the faculty viewpoint.

2. Presidents

The men and women who have been presidents are the ones who have had the major role in the making of decisions that determine the institution's future, as well as its current effectiveness. The preponderant source of information about the president's role is the writings of the presidents themselves. Many have chosen to write on their philosophies of education and have revealed incidentally the parts they played (or sought to play).

Much can be gleaned from the thousands of pages of autobiographies, biographies, reminiscences, and other writings of such presidents as Alderman,[12] Capen,[13] Eliot,[14] Day,[15] Harper,[16] Jordan,[17] Keezer,[18] Kirkland,[19] Lowell,[20] Neilson,[21] Perkins,[22] and

[11] *Educational Record*, 37:285–291, October, 1956.

[12] Dumas Malone, *Edwin A. Alderman*, Doubleday & Company, Inc., New York, 1940.

[13] Samuel P. Capen, *The Management of Universities*, Foster and Stewart, Buffalo, 1953.

[14] Charles W. Eliot, *University Administration*, Houghton Mifflin Company, Boston, 1908.

[15] Edmund Ezra Day, "Role of Administration in Higher Education," *Journal of Higher Education*, 17:339–343, October, 1946.

[16] Thomas Wakefield Goodspeed, *William Rainey Harper, First President of the University of Chicago*, University of Chicago Press, Chicago, 1928.

[17] Edward McNawl Burns, *David Starr Jordan, Prophet of Freedom*, Stanford University Press, Stanford, Calif., 1928.

[18] Dexter M. Keezer, *The Light That Flickers*, Harper & Brothers, New York, 1947.

Wriston.[23] Here the presidents' successes and failures in working on the one hand with trustees and on the other hand with the faculty are revealed. These volumes reveal, too, the techniques that individually these presidents used in striving to mobilize the collaborative effort of both groups, and the extent to which they participated as individuals in the processes of decision making in each area of administration. Yet nowhere has an attempt been made to draw from these rich sources a whole-sided evaluation of the role of the president in the governance of a modern institution of higher education.

The writings of faculty members on the role of the president constitute another valuable source of information on the role of the president. Such an article is the useful statement of W. W. Brickman, entitled "College Presidents' Basic Functions." [24] From the views of the "loyal opposition" come significant insights into what presidents have and have not done, and what faculty members expect them to do—and not to do. Most of these writings are to be found in the periodicals, and particularly in the *Bulletin of the American Association of University Professors.*[25]

A fourth and valuable source is the writings of a few men who have concentrated their attention on the study of college and university administration. Outstanding contributors in this field are William H. Cowley, Thomas R. McConnell, and John Dale Russell; the first two are men who became authorities after having escaped from presidential responsibilities. From different vantage points each has contributed frequently and substantially to the

[19] Edwin Mims, *Chancellor Kirkland of Vanderbilt,* Vanderbilt University Press, Nashville, Tenn., 1940.

[20] A. Lawrence Lowell, *What a University President Has Learned,* The Macmillan Company, New York, 1938.

[21] William Allan Neilson, *The Functions of the University,* Northwestern University, Evanston, Ill., 1943.

[22] John A. Perkins, *Plain Talk from a Campus,* University of Delaware Press, Newark, Del., 1959.

[23] Henry Wriston, "Looking at the College Presidency in Retrospect," *AAUP Bulletin,* 41:504–518, December, 1955.

[24] *School and Society,* 83:65, Feb. 18, 1956.

[25] See, for example, H. L. Donovan, "Changing Conceptions of the College President," *AAUP Bulletin,* 43:40–52, March, 1957.

understanding of administrative problems, and incidentally to the role of the president. Additional contributors, in recent years, to this field are public administrator turned college president and now dean, Donald C. Stone, and Harold W. Stoke, who has written wisely and entertainingly of the role of *The American College President*.[26]

Out of these several sources, however, there is no study that pictures the role of the college president analytically in relation to the institution he serves. The business executive has been subjected to numerous such analyses, as, for example, Melvin T. Copeland's *The Executive at Work*,[27] Ralph J. Cordiner's *New Frontiers for Professional Managers*,[28] and the excellent statements by four businessmen and others in *The Responsibilities of Business Leadership*, a little volume published in 1948.[29] The role of the public administrator similarly has been studied analytically. One early and notable study by Arthur W. Macmahon and John D. Millett provided a whole-sided and analytical study of Federal administrators.[30] Other studies have dealt with governors and city managers. Hopefully, a comparable volume will be produced by Harold Dodds's present effort to study the college presidency.

3. Deans

The heterogeneity of meanings associated with the word *dean* makes an analysis of literature in this field difficult. Our primary concern is with the roles of the academic dean, the dean of faculties, the dean of studies, and of course with the deans of professional and graduate schools, rather than with the deans of men, of women, of students, or of admissions. Four sources yield some information about the role played by these deans in the governance of typical institutions.

The first consists of a few reports of workshops or meetings for

[26] Harper & Brothers, New York, 1959.
[27] Harvard University Press, Cambridge, Mass., 1951.
[28] McGraw-Hill Book Company, Inc., New York, 1956.
[29] Harwood F. Merrill (ed.), Harvard University Press, Cambridge, Mass., 1948.
[30] *Federal Administrators*, Columbia University Press, New York, 1939.

the exchange of experience among deans; notable among these is the report of a workshop at the Catholic University of America in 1956 to consider the function of the "dean of studies" and the reports of meetings of the American Conference of Academic Deans. A second source consists of occasional studies of the administration of groups of denominational schools and the incidental observations they yield about the role of the deans. An especially fruitful source is the biographical and autobiographical material about former deans, such as *Many a Good Crusade*, by Virginia Gildersleeve, former dean at Barnard.[31] Fourth, some of the presidents' writings reveal the contributions made, or the nature of the assistance provided, by the deans who served with these presidents. The role of Ada Comstock as dean of Smith College is well reflected in the Neilson volume, *The Functions of the University*.[32]

From these several sources no definitive picture of the role of the dean in the governance of a modern institution can be put together. As institutions grow and the demands upon the president increase in number and complexity, the role of the dean is likely to be modified materially. Hence, there is an especial need for effective analysis of the evolving role of the dean as a college or university expands in size and in function.

4. Departmental Chairmen

Even more neglected is the role of the department and its chairman. As with the academic dean, the role of the departmental chairman varies widely from institution to institution, and even from department to department. It tends to be (and is among most institutions observed) an influential post in the administrative hierarchy. Hence, the lack of orderly analysis of what the departmental chairmen do and what influence they have is the more grievous. Indeed, only a single volume, by Edward A. Doyle,[33] attempts an orderly analysis of the functions performed by the in-

[31] The Macmillan Company, New York, 1954.
[32] *Op. cit.*
[33] *The Status and Functions of the Departmental Chairman*, The Catholic University of America Press, Washington, D.C., May, 1953.

cumbents of this position, and this analysis is limited to the functioning of departmental chairmen in Catholic institutions.

David Riesman's *Constraint and Variety in American Education* [34] presents a number of insightful and critical observations on the role of departmental chairmen. Riesman, however, does not presume to prescribe the role to be played by the incumbent of this office or the role that is performed in those institutions where the departmental chairmen are especially effective. One article that indirectly contributes to an understanding of this problem of governance is J. K. Hemphill's "Leadership Behavior Associated with Administrative Reputation of College Departments." [35]

5. The Faculty

The role of the faculty, in contrast, has not lacked attention. The AAUP's Committee on "The Place and Function of Faculties in College and University Government" [36] discusses the role that should be played by this pivotal group within institutions of higher education. The committee's review has been thorough and, on the whole, done with commendable objectivity. It is supplemented by the reports of an even greater number of committees set up within particular institutions to review problems that have arisen on the responsibilities of the faculty. [37]

Much that has been written about the role of the faculty has constituted an appeal or demand for "faculty rights" rather than an analytical consideration of the role in which the faculty can most effectively contribute to the functioning of the evolving institution of higher education. This note can be discerned in the reports of the AAUP committee and in the reports of internal faculty committees in a number of institutions. It is the central theme of

[34] University of Nebraska Press, Lincoln, Nebr., 1956.

[35] *Journal of Educational Psychology,* November, 1955. See also, R. E. Heiges, "Functioning Department Heads in Colleges of Medium Size," *Peabody Journal of Education,* November, 1955.

[36] "Final Report on the 1953 Study by Committee T," *AAUP Bulletin,* September, 1955.

[37] For example, *Report of Committee on Faculty Participation in Policy Making,* University of Pittsburgh, November, 1958.

Charles P. Dennison's study, *Faculty Rights and Obligations in Eight Independent Liberal Arts Colleges*.[38]

A more limited number of studies deal with the responsibilities of deans, provosts, and presidents for making the faculty more effective as a teaching and research staff, even as the executives of a business or the officials of a governmental agency accept responsibility for building the capabilities of their staffs. Among the studies that touch on this problem, and the incident problems that arise in relations between the faculty and administrative officers, is the study by John S. Diekhoff of Hunter College, *The Domain of the Faculty in Our Expanding Colleges*.[39] Here the author suggests how, as institutions grow, they can enhance the competence and the role of their expanding faculties. Roy W. Bixler, in his *Institution-Faculty Relations in the College of Integrity*,[40] concerns himself with the relation of the faculty to the administration of an institution. H. M. Wriston included many useful observations on the role of the faculty and its relation to the administration of an institution in his work, *The Nature of the Liberal Arts College*.[41] And Harry J. Carman, formerly dean of Columbia College, pointed out ways in which universities could evoke the "intellectual growth and efficiency" of their faculties.[42]

Still fewer studies focus attention on the positive role that faculties might play in the governance of colleges and universities. The most notable recent contributions to this subject are George Bogert, "Faculty Participation in American University Government"; [43] B. K. Trippet, "The Role of Faculty in College Administration"; [44] Donald C. Stone, "Perspectives of a President on the Rights, Responsibilities, and Relationships of a College Faculty"; [45] and a re-

[38] Bureau of Publications, Teachers College, Columbia University, New York, 1955.

[39] Harper & Brothers, New York, 1956.

[40] Bureau of Publications, Teachers College, Columbia University, New York, 1939.

[41] Lawrence College Press, Appleton, Wis., 1937.

[42] "Campus Issues and Problems," *The Annals*, American Academy of Political and Social Science, 301:46–57, September, 1955.

[43] *AAUP Bulletin*, 31(1):72–82, spring, 1945.

[44] *AAUP Bulletin*, 43(3):484–491, September, 1957.

[45] *Educational Record*, 37:285–291, October, 1956.

port of a work conference sponsored by the American Council on Education (May 7–9, 1957) that dealt with *Faculty-Administration Relationships.*[46] The latter report concluded with a number of notable suggestions on the need for research into the functioning of faculties. It also included worthwhile observations on how faculties can more effectively participate in the governance of institutions while carrying on their primary responsibility for teaching and research.

6. *External Groups*

The social structure and the governance of a college or university are made complex by its relationships to more or less integral groups external to the institution. The parts that make up the whole complex social system that is a college or university include the governing board, the academic and administrative officers, and the faculty—these are *within* the structure. In addition, however, they include the students (who may be regarded as within), the alumni, the professional or academic organizations with which staff members are affiliated, sometimes citizens' advisory committees, the foundations to whom they look for support and counsel, and the state governments by whom they are chartered and by whom many are supported and "supervised."

Of especial importance to the scholar who would weigh the influence of such external groups are three volumes of quite recent origin. The first is, in fact, two volumes: the report of the Committee on Government and Higher Education entitled *The Efficiency of Freedom,*[47] and the committee's staff report entitled *The Campus and the State.*[48] The urgent problem of rationalizing the relations between state colleges and especially the state universities and the agencies of the state governments that provide essential resources and "less essential" controls is nowhere dealt with better than in this staff report.

[46] American Council on Education, Washington, 1958.

[47] Johns Hopkins Press, Baltimore, 1959.

[48] Johns Hopkins Press, Baltimore, 1959. See also *West Virginia University, 1946–1958*, a report covering the administration of Irvin Stewart as president of the university, July 1, 1946, to June 30, 1958.

The second of the three volumes that illuminate the influence of these external groups is Jacques Barzun's *The House of Intellect*.[49] In this volume a single chapter (Chapter 7) offering the author's views on the influence of foundations on educational institutions and on scholars will provoke much disagreement (it does with me!) but is well worth the reading. Finally, the third volume referred to is William K. Selden's *A Struggle over Standards in Higher Education*.[50] It is written in a sprightly style and provides the most temperate and objective analysis of the role of the accrediting association yet to appear.

Two studies, written in rather crusading terms, deal with the role to be played by students. *On Education and Freedom*, by Harold Taylor, formerly president of Sarah Lawrence College, pleads for increased participation of students in the decision making for the colleges they attend.[51] Frances E. Falvey, in her *Student Participation in College Administration*, describes the role she believes students should play in college administration.[52] A rash of recent publications relative to the influence colleges have in changing the values of their students incidentally shed some insights on the extent to which students can and do influence decision making by their "betters." [53]

In the past most of the literature dealing with alumni pictured ways and means of increasing their loyalty and support. More recently, a few articles and studies have dealt with the representa-

[49] Harper & Brothers, New York, 1959.

[50] Harper & Brothers, 1959; see also the very useful compendium on *Accreditation in Higher Education*, organized and edited by Lloyd E. Blauch, formerly Assistant Commissioner for Higher Education; U.S. Department of Health, Education, and Welfare, 1959.

[51] Abelard-Schuman, Ltd., New York, 1954; see also "The World of the American Student," in *Current Issues in Higher Education*, Washington, D.C., 1956, pp. 21–28.

[52] Bureau of Publications, Teachers College, Columbia University, 1952.

[53] This "rash" includes: Philip E. Jacob, *Changing Values in College*, Edward W. Hazen Foundation, New Haven, Conn., 1956; Edward D. Eddy, Jr., *The College Influence on Student Character*, American Council on Education, Washington, 1959; and *Spotlight on the College Student*, a discussion by the problems and policies committee led by David Riesman, Philip E. Jacob, and Nevitt Sanford, American Council on Education, Washington, 1959.

tion of alumni on institutional governing boards, and even fewer with processes of consultation with alumni on such matters of governance as admissions, athletics, programs of expansion, and finance.[54]

THE ADMINISTRATIVE PROCESS

The administrative process, i.e., the manner in which enterprises—private and public—get work done, has been the subject in recent years of an increasing number of articles, books, papers, and reports. Since Mary Parker Follett's essays were published in 1940,[55] there has been a succession of analytical studies on the functioning of enterprises, particularly in industry and government. Recent studies by sociologists, psychologists, and anthropologists have thrown new light on organizations and the motivations and responses of the persons within them that contribute to successful collaborative functioning. Examples of such studies are E. Wight Bakke, *Bonds of Organization;* [56] Robert K. Merton, *Social Theory and Social Structure;* [57] Edward H. Litchfield, "Notes on a General Theory of Administration"; [57a] Theodore Caplow, "The Criteria for Organizational Success"; [58] Philip Selznick, *Leadership in Administration;* [59] James D. Thompson and William J. McEwen, "Organizational Goals and Environment" and "Goal Setting as an Interaction Process"; [60] and Rensis Likert's article entitled "Measuring Organizational Performance." [61]

Recent delving into the administrative process has given increased emphasis to the central significance of decision making.

[54] For example, John S. Diekhoff, "The Alumnus and His Alma Mater," *Association of American Colleges Bulletin,* December, 1957; and Leroy T. Patton, "In Defense of Alumni," *American Mercury,* December, 1954.

[55] Henry C. Metcalf and L. Urwick, *Dynamic Administration,* Harper & Brothers, New York, 1940.

[56] Harper & Brothers, New York, 1950.

[57] The Free Press, Glencoe, Ill., 1957.

[57a] *Administrative Science Quarterly,* June, 1956.

[58] *Social Forces,* October, 1953.

[59] Row, Peterson & Company, Evanston, Ill., 1957.

[60] *American Sociological Review,* February, 1958.

[61] *Harvard Business Review,* March-April, 1958.

Studies of especial value in this area are the relatively early book by Chester Barnard, *The Functions of the Executive*,[62] and Herbert A. Simon's *Administrative Behavior*.[63] More recent contributions to the consideration of this matter are the essays by Simon and Stephen Bailey in *Research Frontiers in Politics and Government*;[64] Robert Dubin (ed.), *Human Relations in Administration*;[65] Chris Argyris, *Personality and Organization*;[66] and Robert H. Roy, "The Administrative Process."[67] There are many other significant articles on related subjects in recent professional journals in the field of public administration and management.

What relevance has this material for the college and university? The best answer is found in John A. Perkins's *Plain Talk from a Campus*, where he declares: "The substance of the discipline known as public administration has much to offer the university or college administrator." He explains that the university is, after all, an organization of persons who jointly strive to accomplish certain common objectives. Like other organizations, particularly agencies with a social purpose, its administrators can derive benefit from what is known and is being discovered about how individuals can work together more efficiently toward a stated goal, i.e., about the science of administration. Few of the works that picture meaningfully the processes of administration lack application to the problem of governing colleges and universities.

Yet the record shows that relatively few of the evolving theories of administration have found their way into the writing about higher institutions. Logan Wilson's *The Academic Man*[68] and his more recent article, "Academic Administration: Its Abuses and Uses,"[69] and some articles like Donald C. Stone's "Perspectives of a President on the Rights, Responsibilities, and Relationships of a College Faculty," reflect the application of some of the newer theo-

[62] Harvard University Press, Cambridge, Mass., 1950.
[63] The Macmillan Company, New York, 1947.
[64] The Brookings Institution, Washington, 1955.
[65] Prentice-Hall, Inc., Englewood Cliffs, N.J., 1951.
[66] Oxford University Press, New York, 1942.
[67] *AAUP Bulletin*, winter, 1955.
[68] Oxford University Press, New York, 1942.
[69] *AAUP Bulletin*, winter, 1955.

ries to the reasoning about the administrative process in the university, but these are exceptions. The most comprehensive—but an unsatisfying attempt because of its addiction to the oldest, most conventional, and outmoded concepts of administration—has been Lloyd S. Woodburne's *Principles of College and University Administration*.[70]

Many persons have written on problems of academic administration—problems of personnel; of accounting, budgeting, and finance; and of physical planning and maintenance. Some who have written with care and thought are Roy J. Deferrari of the Catholic University of America, Daniel L. Marsh of Boston University, Samuel P. Capen of the University of Buffalo, and Edmund Ezra Day of Cornell. One could add to the list almost indefinitely.

But these writings offer little evidence of any effort to see why the academic making and carrying out of decisions proved difficult and what were the obstacles inherent in a university that impeded a solution. Moreover, there is little evidence in this literature that indicates an effort by academic administrators or students of academic administration to explore whether others outside the academic world encountered similar problems. The assumption that the university is different and not subject to assistance from the considered experience of other institutions seems to be the crucial barrier to imaginative development of new and improved means of governance. A related barrier or a cause is the fact that academic administrators are most often teachers who more or less "back in" to administration; they tend to assume that what there is to be known about administration can be picked up as one goes along. The idea of systematic training for administrative posts—an idea generally accepted in business—is not generally accepted, and is even considered bizarre, *in academia*.

INSTITUTIONAL STUDIES

In the final analysis, the governance of a college or university is reflected best by those studies which treat the institution as a

[70] Stanford University Press, Stanford, Calif., 1958.

whole enterprise. It is meaningful to study a segment (the president) or a cross section (the financing problem) of an institution, but it is essential to study the functioning of the institution as a whole if one is to ascertain by whom and how decisions are made and influenced. Four kinds of studies are available that deal with institutions as whole enterprises.

First, there are numerous historical studies of individual institutions (e.g., Philip Alexander Bruce, *The History of the University of Virginia;* [71] James Gray, *University of Minnesota, 1851–1951;* [72] and George Wilson Pierson, *Yale College, an Educational History, 1871–1921* [73]). Their value is limited. They reveal at points the loci of decision-making problems, but more often they record what was done rather than relate why it was done.

A second group of studies are those made in recent years by professional management consultants to determine ways and means of improving the administration of the college or university.[74] Approximately two hundred such studies have been made since World War II. They are concerned, in principal part, with the practices of the noneducational units in a college operation. There is little attempt in most studies to evaluate the educational mission of the institution or the organization of the faculty and its part in decision making.

Appraisals of institutions by teams of educators, brought in by a board of education or a college to study its functioning in relation to local higher educational needs, have been commonplace. A study such as that on *Higher Education in Kansas City* reveals an evaluation by experts of the community's educational needs at the university level and how they are being met, and suggests how the University of Kansas City could meet them better. The primary focus on the community's needs makes these studies effective mir-

[71] The Macmillan Company, New York, 1920.

[72] University of Minnesota Press, Minneapolis, 1951.

[73] Yale University Press, New Haven, Conn., 1952.

[74] For a statement generally descriptive of the subject matter of such studies see H. J. Heneman, "Opportunities for Improved Management in Higher Education," chap. 6 in Dexter M. Keezer (ed.), *Financing Higher Education: 1960–1970,* McGraw-Hill Book Company, Inc., New York, 1959.

rors of the influence of local forces on internal decision making.

"Self-studies" by members of the staffs—faculty and administrative—are sometimes more revealing of problems of institutional governance and their handling. Among such studies are the report of the president's committee at Columbia University, entitled *The Educational Future of the University*,[75] and the *Report to the Middle States Association of Colleges and Secondary Schools, of the Pennsylvania State University*.[76] Their authors were careful to analyze the university in its setting and to assess the ecological influences on the organization of the university. It offers a stimulating analysis of the goals that should be sought by this particular university and many sidelights on the responsibilities in other institutions of trustees, academic and administrative officers, and faculty.

Finally, a quite recent and notable contribution to thinking about the organization and governance of a total institution has come from Edward H. Litchfield in the form of an article entitled "Organization in Large American Universities." [77] It deals with the organization of the disciplinary departments and their relation to one another, and to the professional and graduate schools. Here he advances thoughts about a central problem of academic governance which is recognized by other students but attacked by few college or university administrators.

If the foregoing pages force the reader to conclude that the scholar in this field must glean bits and pieces from many and varied sources, then they have served their purpose. If these pages emphasize the disturbing lack of sophisticated analysis of the functioning of our colleges and universities, then surely they will have served a useful purpose. If they fail to picture for the would-be scholar the real fun and adventure to be had in seeking out the stuff from which a better understanding of the governance of colleges and universities can be built, then the writing of these pages has failed.

[75] Columbia University, New York, 1957.

[76] Data submitted for consideration of the Commission on Institutions of Higher Education, Middle States Association of Colleges and Secondary Schools, Sept. 1, 1955.

[77] *Journal of Higher Education*, 30:353–364, October, 1959.

INDEX